"Character determines whether a person succeeds in life or not. High IQ alone is not enough, leadership is not domination but the art of persuading people to work toward a common goal. This requires high interpersonal skills and social intelligence."
—Mr Goh Chok Tong
Prime Minister of Singapore

"Psychologists agree that IQ contributes only about 20 percent of the factors that determine success. A full 80 percent comes from other factors, including what I call emotional intelligence."
—Dr Daniel Goleman, author of
Emotional Intelligence

"The competitive edge will belong not to those who use computers but to those who know how to inspire more productivity and excellence from each individual. We are about to enter a new century of unprecedented human growth and development. We must re-examine and re-evaluate the way we think, the way we respond to life's daily challenges in what will be a time of even more astonishing change."
—Dr Denis Waitley, author of
Empires of the Mind

"There is no true success without emotional success, yet, more than 3,000 emotions that we have words to describe, the average person experiences only about a dozen different ones in the course of an average week. We must remember that this does not reflect our emotional capacity, but rather the limitations of our present patterns of focus and physiology."
—Anthony Robbins, author of
Awc

D1492829

"Self-observation is essential for self-growth. You must first understand the motives for your own actions in order to understand others."
—Chin-Ning Chu, author of
Thick Face Black Heart

"Valuing the difference is the essence of synergy—the mental, the emotional, the psychological differences between people. And the key to valuing those differences is to realize that all people see the world, not as it is, but as they are."
—Stephen R Covey, author of
The Seven Habits of Highly Effective People

"Met Life found that salesmen who tested high for optimism sold 37 percent more insurance that their pessimistic brethren their first two years on the job."
—Martin Seligman, author of
Learned Optimism

EQ
EMOTIONAL INTELLIGENCE

IN THE WORKPLACE

*bridging the gap between what
we know and what we do*

Dr Patricia Patton

Thank you to Diana Thompson, my editor, for all of her support and editorial guidance and to SNP Publishers for believing in the books and for making them a reality.

© 1997 Patricia Patton

Published by
SNP Publishing Pte Ltd
under their Raffles Editions imprint
162 Bukit Merah Central
#06-3545
Singapore 150162

First published 1997

Cover design by Albert Tan

ISBN 9971 0 0770 3

Set in 11/15 point Goudy (EPB)

Printed by JBW Printers & Binders Pte Ltd

About the Author

Dr Denis Waitley, the eminent consultant for Fortune 500 companies and author of many best sellers, such as *Empires of the Mind* wrote:

"Dr Patricia Patton is a colleague for whom I have the greatest respect. She has a proven track record of excellence in academic, government, institutional organizations and the private sector. I have served with her on the President of the United States' Council for Vocational Education and have attended her television, university and corporate presentations. Dr Patton is bright, articulate, creative, demonstrates integrity and provides real-life action strategies for effective human productivity and empowerment."

Dr Patton is a popular motivational speaker, seminar presenter and management consultant on emotional intelligence and personal development for organizations that want to improve their performance, productivity, profitability, staff retention and team morale. Her rich and diverse professional background is a result of working in the private and public sectors as well as serving in leadership and management level positions. This, coupled with her academic training in education and speaking experience make her an expert in emotional intelligence and human development. Based on this accumulated expertise Dr Patton possesses a clear insight into the skills needed for organizations to be successful and competitive in the 21st century.

Dr Patton has served as a Development Consultant and Principal Advisor to the Prime Minister of Papua New Guinea, Consultant in the United States Department of Education, Chairperson of Michigan State University's National Alumni Association Board of Directors, Senior

Vice-President of a Regional Chamber of Commerce in the United States, Vice-President for United Way in the United States, and Teacher and Administer for an urban school system.

Her knowledge and passion for team-building, developing relevant organizational values and norms, along with her emphasis on cultivating high individual and group emotional intelligence is gaining considerable presence in the Asia Pacific region.

An array of services are offered by Dr Patton for corporations and business organizations to increase their individual and team emotional competencies that are necessary for them to obtain professional excellence. Her six EQ services include:

- Individual and small group coaching for leadership, management, and employees to more effectively balance their personal skills with their professional capabilities.
- EQ seminars and motivational presentations.
- Management consultant services for sustaining EQ implementation.
- Managing internationalization from an EQ perspective seminars.
- Administering an EQ personal development instrument for self-understanding and development.
- EQ seminars, coaching and consulting for educational leaders and practitioners.

For any additional information, please contact Dr Patricia Patton at:
International Business Proactivity (IBP) Pte Ltd
Riverwalk Galleria #26-02
20 Upper Circular Road
Singapore 058416
Tel: (65) 536 0628; Fax: (65) 536 0610; E-mail: ibp@pacific.net.sg

To my husband, Yann A Meunier,
whose love and wisdom have enriched my life.
To God,
whose care and guidance have been my tower of strength.

CONTENTS

PART FOUR: EQ WORKPLACE SKILLS

INTRODUCTION

Why EQ in the Workplace?

Imagine being invisible for a moment and walking into a party full of business people you have never met before. As you saunter around the room you hear all kinds of conversations and observe many non-verbal expressions. It becomes quite clear that some people are comfortable and some are not. It is also apparent that as human beings we feel many emotions that result in jealousies, hurts, anger, frustration, happiness, anxiety and fear. From feelings, we manifest behaviours which can be expressions of openness, enthusiasm, hostility, apathy, mistrust, enjoyment and friendliness. It is in the interactions and relationship building that emotions play a critical role. They are also paramount when we are making decisions, solving problems and using our intellectual endowments to obtain a goal. At these moments and others, having emotional intelligence (EQ) is a major asset.

Based on his extensive and behavioural research, Dr Daniel Goleman has shown the significant role emotions play in our mental life and that we actually have two minds: one that thinks and one that feels. Our emotional mind has the authority to override our thinking in times of passion and when emotionally upset. According to Dr Goleman, psychologists agree that IQ contributes only about 20 percent of the factors that determine success. A full 80 percent comes from other factors, including emotional intelligence. This breakthrough research has tremendous implications for the business environment and for the way we manage ourselves and others. He cites that EQ includes such traits as:

- self-awareness
- mood management
- self-motivation
- impulse control
- people skills

In light of this new and significant research it is now clear that IQ alone is not the factor which turns a person successful. It is the blending of both IQ and EQ which can make a difference in achieving success in the workplace.

Those of us who subscribe to the cognitive scientist view that the mind is a matter of storing and processing information into facts would find it difficult to entertain the notion that we have another mind which feels and has more power than IQ to make us effective or ineffective.

EQ means simply, using your emotions effectively to achieve goals, develop productive relationships and attain success in the workplace.

In a knowledge-based work environment there is a propensity for developing skills that are highly technical and focused. Training programs that direct attention to building professional skills are most popular. The more information we have, the better able we are to gain the edge over competitors. Many organizations are looking to tap the intellectual capabilities of employees to increase their information power. This also enhances productivity. It is widely believed that success lies in the ability to use IQ to understand and synthesize a large amount of data and that emotions have no real function. The education community is assisting organizations to perpetuate the philosophy of intellect being the driving force behind success in life.

In the world today, it is important to have some technical knowledge or know-how in order to perform in a job. However, even with all this knowledge and information floating around there still remains real concerns within the workplace and more importantly, with the people that must work within these organizations. The following are some of the problems that cause concern to individuals and organizations. Do you face any of them?

Common Problems

1. Individuals are not happy with themselves or where they are working.
2. Individuals do not take personal responsibility for what they do.
3. Individuals experience health problems because of their inability to adjust to demands within the workplace.
4. Individuals feel stress and lack an interest in their jobs.
5. Individuals loose their passion, excitement and self-motivation.
6. Certain employees cause unhappiness among their colleagues as a result of their behaviour and attitude.
7. Managers give ineffective feedback to employees.
8. Managers find it difficult to build synergetic teams.
9. Customers are not satisfied with the service and look for alternatives.
10. Families suffer as a result of job pressures.
11. Organizations experience problems with retention and staff morale.
12. Organizations experience problems with productivity.

1. Self-Reflection Questions

1. How many of the problems stated above are you concerned with?
2. How many points could you add to the list?
3. How many of the problems have to do with technical knowledge or skill?
4. How many problems have to do with personal competence or interpersonal abilities?
5. How many people fail because they don't understand themselves or other people?
6. How many organizations suffer because they do not recognize or appreciate their employees or customers?

There are some people who would argue that you do not have to be popular or even effective in dealing with others to succeed in life:

This is true if you mean accomplishing at the detriment of others or at the expense of your own personal happiness.

This is true if you only equate money, power and material possessions with success.

This is true if you hurt others, but care little because you believe everyone should take care of themselves.

This is true if you aren't interested in your integrity, compassion for others, and building a happy life for yourself as well for other people.

This is true if you aren't interested in creating or leaving a legacy where people flourish as a result of knowing you.

When examining success more carefully many individuals would contend that it goes far beyond having obtained power, money or status.

This is evident by looking closely at the lives of people who have all of the above and are still unhappy. The person with a high IQ who does not have friends and lives without making a difference can end up lonely and disillusioned. The employee who knows his or her job expertly but can't relate well with their children or co-workers will not form meaningful relationships. To be truly successful in life requires a blend of IQ and EQ.

Employees must have personal skills in order to enhance and complement their professional abilities. Some of the benefits of harmonizing IQ and EQ are that individuals will be able to:

- work better with their employees
- become better team members
- feel self-confident and empowered to achieve their goals
- handle conflicts more effectively
- provide better service
- communicate more effectively
- lead and manage employees with a heart and head philosophy
- create organizations that have high integrity, values and behavioural standards

IQ is an unchangeable genetic factor which we are born with. EQ is not. We can improve it with commitment, practice, knowledge and will. The foundation for enhancing our EQ is in knowing ourselves.

Self-awareness is the essential ingredient for bringing clarity and understanding to our actions. It is the starting point for personal development. It is at this point that EQ building can begin. A conduit to self-awareness is responsibility and courage. These factors are crucial to personal change and when facing up to aspects of ourselves that aren't pleasant.

EQ is the bridge between what we know and what we do. The higher our EQ, the better skilled we are at doing what we know is right.

For example, most people would agree that it is not effective to lose one's temper and shout at another person. There is nothing to be gained but shame, hurt feelings, embarrassment, and guilt. Nonetheless, educated and highly intelligent people still succumb to anger. Why? Because although they know it isn't appropriate intellectually, their emotional mind tells them something different. Passions often have the ability to override logic. Lust and anger can out-talk reasoning when allowed. Interpersonal success which is derived from having emotional intelligence will be one of the most important skills for the 21st century. Emotions add depth and richness to our lives. Without feelings our actions would be more like a computer, thinking but without passion. Building support for an important project and merging with the emotions of others are important skills within the workplace.

EQ Challenge for the Workplace: What Does it Mean to the Bottom Line?

If managers were asked to identify the challenges their organizations had to address in order to achieve their profit goals, the answers would be different, but the main themes would be the same:

1. The need to retain positive, competent and productive employees who are able to meet and exceed the expectations of customers.
2. The need to create organizations that are service-oriented, quality focused and able to deal with the challenges of rapidly changing working environments.

A bottom line factor is to gain and maintain the competitive edge and to use creative strategies to tap new markets. Meeting these challenges and other specialized needs require employees to have:

- the intellectual ability to carry out various levels of responsibility
- the ability to work with people to accomplish the organization's goals
- the emotional maturity to deal with change, challenge, uncertainty and conflict

Far too often, managers are preoccupied with an employee's ability to perform their job well. They assume this can be accomplished by technical training and on-the-job experience. This is only half-true. The half that is usually missing is the EQ portion where in order to achieve profit margins and bottom line results we need to ensure that employees can:

- manage their emotions and the emotions of others
- recognize whether problems are emotional or rational
- maximize the use of positive emotions such as optimism, persistence, and hope in the pursuit of a goal
- keep self-motivated and self-disciplined to maintain quality and productivity
- feel empathy and concern for others
- exercise integrity and loyalty

These are not technical skills but human competencies which can be cultivated if an organization is willing to make them a priority. To excel in a job and increase performance means applying emotional intelligence in customer relationships, team efforts, and self-efficacy.

The best place to harness this is in the workplace. Individuals who possess EQ are the catalysts for building relationships in an organization. They are the stars who create a forum for employee bonding.

The link between EQ and IQ for increased profits and subsequent bottom line achievement can be accomplished by bridging what we know with what we do: using the combination of mind and heart when dealing with all matters. This means utilizing the emotional part of our brain with the thinking part in a partnership to ensure the best of both worlds within our minds. This alliance is formidable and will increase the bottom line by increased productivity, synergetic teams, happy customers, effective managers, and organizations that are harmonious and service-oriented. The following are examples of an EQ bridge.

(1) **As managers are trained in new techniques,** offer them an opportunity to develop their self-awareness and emotional competence. One way of doing this is to create a space for them to discuss the various emotions they use when working with their subordinates. Assist them in recognizing the feelings in others, and the ways to stimulate positive feelings and discourage negative and unproductive behaviours. Likewise, when employees learn a new skill or receive a different position, work with them to develop the emotional tools necessary to function effectively and identify the personal requirements needed to be successful.

(2) **Ascertain whether the core values, mission statement and vision complement the day-to-day operational policies,** procedures, performance appraisals and job descriptions. Develop a process for determining how people are treated, and the kind of behavioural standards expected and used. Also, learn why employees stay and why they leave the organization. Measure whether management technique is more important than a manager's personal qualities. Make them more balanced.

(3) **Blend professional knowledge with emotional intelligence in determining how to best work with customers and co-workers.** Set up systems for helping employees overcome fear, insecurity, and uncertainty by making sure they understand why they have these

feelings and determine the best way to channel them. For reassigned or unmotivated employees, time should be spent to discover what they are feeling and how to help them get a better grounding for increasing their level of productivity.

(4) **Determine what is the organizational culture and leadership type in order to assess** if it is demanding professional growth at the expense of personal enrichment.

(5) **Ensure that change strategies and other innovations** which require employees to do something different is coupled with opportunities for them to understand and discuss their feelings and emotional responses. This will ensure that they are in sync with the demands being placed on them professionally. By taking time to know what your employees are feeling and thinking doesn't mean you are running a psychological service, it means that you recognize the importance of blending logic and emotion.

(6) **Pay particular attention to what is done just as closely as to what is said.** The best planning will fall apart if promises are not met, unwritten rules contradict the written ones, trust is broken, or employees feel powerless to implement their job responsibilities. Be careful not to worry more about the function of the job than the people who must carry out their tasks.

(7) **Does the financial reward fairly match the depth and breath of the job** which the employee must accomplish?

(8) **Does a behaviour, attitude or expression add value, or diminish value from the job performance?** In other words, are we overly anxious, impatient, angry, shy or frustrated; or are we self-motivated, open, confident, disciplined and optimistic?

(9)   Are decisions made with integrity, empathy and consideration?

(10) Is achieving bottom line results more important than the process by which the outcome is obtained?

The above examples illustrate how EQ is an integral part of professional activities. There are very few areas in office or other work environments where EQ isn't a major factor in determining the quality of relationships and the quantity of work.

Why a Balance Between IQ And EQ?

The research of Dr Goleman demonstrates that our brain actually has two minds, one that thinks and the other that feels. The emotional mind was developed before the thinking one, giving further relevance to the importance of understanding ourselves. Since passions give breadth and depth to our existence, they also have the capability to undermine our rational and logic mind. This means that we can actually do the opposite of what we know to be right. For example, impatience can snowball into anger, causing an inappropriate reaction. Once our rational mind gets back in control, we often wonder why we reacted the way we did. To understand the power of how we feel and the behaviours that follow are at the core of emotional intelligence. These factors can determine how effective or ineffective we are in implementing our professional work responsibilities.

The winners of the 21st century will be people who can balance IQ with EQ. Mr Goh Chok Tong, the Prime Minister of Singapore very eloquently expressed the importance of EQ when he stated:

"Character determines whether a person succeeds in life or not. High IQ alone is not enough ... leadership is not domination but the art of persuading people to work toward a common goal. This requires high interpersonal skills and social intelligence ... I absorbed a heavy dose of emotional intelligence at Raffles Institution. It built my character. It gave me the emotional gravitas to lead."

Mr Goh Chok Tong
Prime Minister of Singapore

Leaders who exemplify EQ are often the most loved because their contributions go further than doing the right thing. They make a difference in the lives of people and because of them others are better off. Personal leadership is where everything starts in life. It means that intellectual skills coupled with character, temperament, and attitude are developed to make contributions in your professional and personal life. Without a balance between what we know and what we do, we fall victim to:

- making heartless decisions
- stifling our own career growth
- hurting the people we care about as well as co-workers
- decreasing our effectiveness with people
- limiting our personal power to strive for greater challenges and thus receive better rewards
- acting in ways that decrease our potential and undermine our sense of self

The 21st century will demand much more of us than any century before because it will be a time when the limits of human potential will be pushed. We will have to live and work together in a different way which will require interdependence and pooling talents to keep up with the continually changing workplace. We will need to re-learn some human relation skills that were lost with the invention of the computer and E-mail which have created isolation and impersonal communication.

No longer will we be able to hide our true natures behind technology because competition and commercialism will shed light on our characters. Through global communication our customers, colleagues and competitors will know what we know and what we don't know.

What is the advantage we have over technology? It is our ability to interrelate with each other, build co-operative relationships, and master our own behaviours. We have the potential of discipline, compassion, emotional literacy, and the ability to understand others. These attributes will help us survive and prosper within an organization. But more at risk is the survival of our global society and the legacy we leave our children. What we know and what we do will be key factors in determining if we leave them a world full of inept adults unable to work together, overambitious, uncaring, and unable to deal with the pressure and challenges of their lives, or we leave them a world filled with emotionally attuned adults, understanding and respecting one another, knowing how to work together to build a better world and genuinely caring for humankind.

Some in the business world may say EQ in the workplace is a soft issue, better left to the home or religious sphere. They may believe that it is not "hard" enough as a business strategy or the financial bottom-line world of materialism. I propose that it is the reverse. Not developing and leading organizations that are emotionally able to deal with the challenges and pressures of the global marketplace means leaving organizations in a soft position. Making the workplace synergetic and truly empowering is to establish hard-core values that will not bend in the slightest breeze and where people know without question they are valued. It includes leadership which has integrity and the know-how to create environments that build quality of life, rather than depleting from it. What better place to infuse the ideals of EQ than the workplace. Where is there a better opportunity, a bigger audience, a more influential place in which to develop people personally and professionally and to encourage better homes for our children and for ourselves than in the business environment?

Management books on leadership and employee development often interpret from the core of who we are as people. The inner-child who is still throwing tantrums although a manager; or the inner child who sulks and gets even rather than learning to resolve disagreements appropriately. These individuals will learn to intellectualize management techniques and perhaps even use them, but these techniques will not make them into individuals who empower and support others. There must be a point where we incorporate what we know intellectually with what we do emotionally so that our words and actions reflect who we really want to be. Too often, people act through learned experience and repetition. This can hurt those who have to endure the tyranny of emotionally illiterate people who gain power without knowing how to manage themselves or others. Knowing how to manage our moods and balance them with our logical side when dealing with challenges and adversity will help us build positive and productive relationships as we move toward accomplishing our goals.

Personal development and human relation skills will be two important areas for businesses to cultivate in the 21st century. It is time for us to assume responsibility for ourselves and take the initiative in developing working environments, ready to deal with the challenges of an increasingly competitive and technologically driven global marketplace. Before we can accomplish this we must understand our emotional make-up and how to manage ourselves in good times as well as bad. The strategies and ideas in this book are derived from years of experience and research into why some people seem to know how to relate to others, while others do not. Balancing our intellect with our emotions is a challenge worth pursuing at a personal, corporate, and societal level.

An +EQ/–EQ Confrontation

As you read the exercise below which is based on a true story, write down on the space provided an EQ+ when it was utilized and an EQ– when emotions were not effectively managed. Also, write down the emotions you believe should have been used to increase EQ.

Exercise

Mary was a young and talented woman whom the executive team was grooming for a leadership position. They had given her the assignment to provide them with an independent report on whether the company should proceed with a new and innovative project. Richard, a senior manager and longtime employee of the company was the project leader and believed it should be adopted by the company. He had visions of heading up this new unit if it were accepted.

Mary completed her research, and discovered data which proved that the project would not be cost-effective or productive. It was her conclusion that the project should not be implemented. Richard was developing a case to force his proposal through and was unaware of the findings in Mary's report. In his desire to win this project, he tried to cover up its negative aspects.

At the presentation meeting with the executive team, Richard began his lengthy presentation. He spoke passionately about the need to implement the project and explained why it would hurt the company if they didn't go along with his plan. After he finished the executive team asked a few questions which he quickly answered with short punchy comments. He used his familiarity with the team and his long-standing employment with the company to weather any negative questions.

The executive team leader asked for Mary's report. As she proceeded to dispute Richard's findings, he began to turn red. His body language indicated that he wasn't happy with the report and in the middle of her remarks, he jumped up out of his seat and stated that her report was filled with a pack of lies and how dare an upstart like her challenge his professional knowledge. He had been working long before Mary was even born!

---

1. What +EQ or –EQ aspects are operating here?

_____

_____

_____

_____

_____

2. What emotions are present?

_____

_____

_____

_____

The team asked Richard to sit down and allow Mary to finish her report. The team leader indicated he would have time to respond later. Mary hesitated but continued to give her findings in a professional manner. As she began to refute his cost projections Richard demanded to speak. The team leader, seeing his anger, decided to let him address her data. Instead of discussing the actual information, he carried on about Mary's inexperience, lack of integrity, and team spirit in working with him to prepare a joint proposal. He further went on to say that she should not be allowed to present her report because it lacked correct information. The longer he talked, the louder his voice became and the angrier the tone.

---

1. What +EQ or –EQ aspects are operating here?

2. What emotions are present?

As Richard continued, Mary felt herself becoming very uncomfortable. The executive team darted their eyes back and forth between Mary and Richard as if they were watching a tennis match, not quite knowing what to think of this turn of events.

Mary felt that more was at stake than the report, Richard was challenging her character. Mary composed herself and channelled the impulse to defend herself and interrupt his tirade. In order to do so, she forced herself to feel sorry that a man of such stature and ability didn't have the emotional maturity to deal with the matter more professionally. Richard's remarks were now becoming a monologue and repetitious. The executive team leader finally could not take any more and, interrupting him, asked Mary for a rebuttal. She stood tall and straight, exuding confidence and continued with her remarks. She kept her comments strictly to the rationale of her report making no unsubstantiated remarks, nor did she address the personal attacks at that time. Mary addressed only Richard's professional comments relative to the validity of the report.

As she continued, the blood vessels in Richard's neck looked as if they were going to burst. He experienced an emotional hijacking where his reasoning gave way to emotions. He began to shout. Mary, still in control but irritated, informed the team that Richard's unprofessionalism and personal attacks on her were becoming abusive. Although she had a few other items to present she felt that it was not practical for her to continue. She drew their attention to the sections that would conclude her presentation and asked if she could be excused from the meeting.

---

1. What +EQ or –EQ aspects are operating here?

_____

_____

_____

_____

_____

_____

_____

---

2. What emotions are present?

_____

_____

_____

_____

_____

_____

_____

Conclusion

Mary was asked back to the meeting after a short recess and the atmosphere was different. After having been confronted by his boss, Richard was less emotionally charged, although his anger went underground which could be seen again by his body language. Mary was allowed to finish her report. The outcome was that her findings were accepted, but the downside of her victory was that Richard would play a major role in overseeing its implementation. This was his reward for being a member of the old boys' network and for having known all of the decision-makers for years. They recognized Mary's talents, but they also honoured Richard by their support. Mary knew she was going to need all of her emotional skills and abilities to deal with Richard who was now an enemy in her own camp, at least until the program was implemented.

1. What is your reaction to the conclusion?

    _____

    _____

    _____

    _____

    _____

2. What advice would you give to Mary on how to handle her emotions during this time?

    _____

    _____

    _____

    _____

3. How effective was the executive team in handling the situation. Were they an +EQ or –EQ group?

    _____

    _____

    _____

    _____

The situation proved to be a mixed blessing for Mary. By having to work daily with a man who disliked her professionally, she learned more about her strengths as a person and it sharpened her professional skills. The experience helped her in future work environments and in dealing with other toxic people of varying degrees. During her working association, she also learned from Richard's years of experience. This could have also worked the opposite way if she had not used her thinking and emotional mind in harmony with one another. When this is achieved you have two powerful allies. Unfortunately for many, this is not the case and the emotional mind wins out.

The inability to deal with emotions in the workplace is the underlining cause of *anomie* (where there is no accepted and reinforced values or standards of behaviour present) in organizational environments which cause misery to employees. If you doubt this statement, just observe how many colleagues feel satisfied, valued, and secure with their boss or peers. This is not to say that employees should feel great about their work and the office staff every day. But when they feel bad about themselves and their work due to poor relationships more often than they feel positive, this is a cause of concern.

The challenge for all of us working in corporate and other organizational settings is to bridge the gap between what we know and what we do. Richard knew intellectually that his actions were not appropriate, but his habit of getting his way by intimidating, coupled with his lack of experience in having to debate with a young woman were too much for him to take. It stretched his limit.

Bullying is not to be confused with gaining support or using aboveboard methods to influence people. Bullying is when a person knowingly sets out to sabotage or destroy another colleague. Bullies pride themselves on win/lose scenarios with them always the victor.

When someone does something grossly unprofessional it stands out like a sore thumb. It can also be said that subtle behaviour and attitude can be just as dangerous. Richard exposed his emotional inaptitude and insensitivity publicly. However, there are many people who would not expose themselves in that way and who prefer to work underground. This is more disconcerting because it can hit you at any time. However, we can triumph even over the bully who inhabits our workplace as well. The first place to start is to uncover the mysteries of our emotional side. By becoming self-aware, we will be more attuned to our own emotions and the emotions of others. This will come in handy when we find ourselves getting caught up in the feelings of the moment and forgetting what we know to be right. It will help us to rethink our habits and past experiences of interacting which may have become outdated and ineffective maps. We are all subject to times of not managing ourselves effectively, misreading the emotional cues in others, or not empathizing. It takes emotional intelligence, discipline, maturity, and the will to change self-defeating habits and toxic behaviours to create inner peace and interpersonal competence. The E to our EQ is to Empower others to grow and work at their best as a member of a synergetic team. This is vital to the well-being of organizational life and takes the efforts of everyone to make it a reality.

PART ONE
REBUILDING OUR INNER WALL

THE ARCHITECTURAL DESIGN OF THE EQ ORGANIZATION

To develop emotional intelligence within the workplace requires first creating an organizational plan which will outline the architectural design. This means projecting:

1. A kind of infrastructure including such items as mission statement, vision, goals, and financial targets that will sustain the organization's direction.
2. Values and behaviours that will provide the foundation to keep the organization strong.
3. Policies and procedures that will provide the bricks and mortar to build a proper structure.
4. Empowerment opportunities and team motivational strategies that will provide the important details to add class and distinction to the organization.
5. A cultural atmosphere that will illuminate and enhance the organization's aesthetics.

Achieving an EQ organizational design necessitates creating a builder's paradigm among employees to encourage the blending of personal and professional skills. This will enable organizations to address the challenges, stresses, and fears of its employees and the adversity that it creates. The prerequisite for accomplishing an EQ workplace is for each employee to develop an effective inner wall to provide him with the strength, wisdom, and skills to deal with everyday work situations. The value of doing this is it serves as a catalyst for:

(1)   **Empowering yourself and others** to create relationships and work

together for a common end result, rather than working apart for hidden and individual agendas.

(2) **Dealing with the enormity of global competition,** information explosion, and technological advances, all which results in a stronger need for not losing our humanity in all of these advancements.

(3) **Understanding people more** and increasing positive and productive interactions.

Employees who can respond to the needs of others in a personal way will rise above the technocrats who can only use the technology from an impersonal perspective. EQ literate people will eventually win out because of their effectiveness in relating to customers, dealing with uncertainty, and maintaining motivation. This will determine their success and ultimately the organization's survival.

1.   Building Blocks

Developing emotional intelligence is like being a builder. It requires:

- Knowing what it is that you desire to create (the personal change that is necessary), the problems that you will encounter (what behaviours, attitudes and temperament are holding you back), the tools needed (the resources that are available to help you grow as a person) and an idea of what the finished product will look like.
- Know-how which comes from studying, learning from others and your own mistakes (utilizing your intellectual knowledge with wisdom that comes from experience).

To be an EQ builder takes a lot of work because of the layer upon layer of protective walls we create to hide our fears, pride, selfishness, and stubbornness against changing. Even when we make improvements, some of us fall back into old habits because it is easier and safer than struggling with new attitudes and behaviours. To become a builder of our own emotions and behaviours takes four building blocks:

Building Block 1: AWARENESS

When this is achieved, we become aware of who we are, how we affect people in our lives, and we listen to our inner voice which tells us if we are personally successful or not. Often we drown out this voice with denials, protestations, anger, self-pity, and other forms of avoidance in order not to deal with our real need to re-examine the way we do things. Some of us even look for people who will tell us what we want to hear, rather than what is true. In order to build a better inner wall we must first recognize that one is needed. This wall must be flexible enough so that it is:

- open, willing to be repaired when necessary
- sturdy in its foundation and will not topple in the slightest storm
- strong with conviction in doing what is right

Building Block 2: ACCEPTING RESPONSIBILITY

To know oneself is to also take responsibility for our good and bad side. This does not mean that we resign ourselves to living with negative and unproductive moods. We should accept the fact that we make mistakes and acknowledge a more positive way of acting and feeling. We can also take responsibility for building a better inner wall so that we may change the course of our actions.

Building Block 3: Commitment

In order to become a builder we have to make a commitment in working daily to construct an inner wall that is positive, effective, and personally fulfilling. This means having faith in our ability to change into a more effective, and positive self. By making a commitment we must weather the change process even when it is painful and difficult.

Building Block 4: Action

We can't build anything if we do not take the first step which is to design our blueprint, organize our resources, and begin the process of producing. Action means doing. To accomplish any goal involves generating an energy and enthusiasm for achievement. The four building blocks show the path toward rebuilding our emotional intelligence.

The Builder's Concept in EQ: Five Building Tools

The EQ builder's tools spur us into action and to take initiative in developing personal leadership for making a difference in the way we feel and interact with other people. The interpersonal skills are a key to success in the workplace. The five builder's tools presented require us to:

1. DEMONSTRATE

My father used to say, "the proof of the pudding is in the eating". How we feel about ourselves and what we think of others comes across in our actions. If we say we like someone, how do we demonstrate it?

I remember a CEO from a successful company once told me that he couldn't understand why his employees didn't believe him when he said he appreciated their work. He gave them raises as directed by their contracts and organized an annual Christmas party. However, feedback always showed that his employee's didn't believe that they were valued at the office and the turnover rate was high. After careful analysis within his company, I discovered that most of his managers did not feel he cared about them. He rarely asked about their lives, didn't know when tragedy or joy entered their universe, and hardly talked with them when he saw them in the hallway. It was business first and only. His gestures of increases in their pay and the Christmas party were seen as only tokens which had no real value. My suggestion to him was to get to know his managers and staff more personally. This philosophy was "lead by example" and turn the organization into a caring one where employees knew that they were also viewed as people. He was dismayed that he hadn't taken into consideration the feelings of his employees and set out to change the situation. The first step was for his employees to get to know him as a person and he in turn opened himself up to them. As a result, the high turnover decreased by over 60 percent and the environment became one of team synergy and trust.

Demonstrating our feelings can be productive, or misleading. Some people have perfected the art of deception adding drama to their professional lives. It is difficult to know what they really mean and we often fall victim to their outward appearance. The key to dealing with people whose motives are hard to determine is to use our gut-level feelings. This is our intuition which warns us of danger. During the early days of man, this tool was used as a baseline for action. In our sophisticated world we have cast aside our gut feelings. However, when developed this tool can determine the difference between winning, losing, or making mistakes.

This inability to manage our emotions or to identify how we feel, can result in misunderstandings or our being labelled as someone we are not. The level of our emotional intelligence will determine how effectively we demonstrate our emotions. Feeling something, but not showing it, can be frustrating to those around you. For men, not showing love or empathy can cause hurt feelings and rejection within personal relationships. For women, accepting abusive emotions from others can be destructive to physical health and mental well-being.

Learning the art of effective EQ demonstration is a skill which can be cultivated by utilizing the following strategies:

(1)   **Analyse.** This means analyse your emotions when faced with a variety of situations. For example, when you are criticized or become angry, ask yourself the following questions:

> "How does this information or situation make me feel?"
> "What happens to my body when I hear these remarks?"
> "What goes through my mind?"
> "What is my self-talk?"
> "What worries me most?"
> "How do I react?"

(2)   **Identify.** This means identify the correct emotion you are feeling. Often we become confused and misjudge the real emotion we are experiencing. We can't deal with our feelings if we incorrectly or unintentionally label them wrongly. A starting point would be to ask yourself right when an event happens this one major question: "Am I worried or upset by what is happening?" Usually we are either worried or upset that as a result of an event something will

ensue that will be negative for us. In a work situation, if the boss yells at you in front of others, you are upset because you believe he disrespects you or that others will think badly of you. It is not the yelling that is upsetting, but what you perceive to be the reason behind the yelling and what others might think of you which matters the most. If you changed your thinking and said these thoughts to yourself when your boss started yelling your whole outlook on the situation may be different, thus your emotional response. Try and tell yourself: "How immature and unprofessional they look and how sorry I feel for someone in their position not being able to control their emotions." By thinking this, you will shift the focus away from yourself and onto the person who deserves to receive the spotlight in this instance.

(3)   **Manage.** This means manage your emotions when needed. Either we are the master or the slave of our emotions. In EQ demonstration, it is imperative to know how to analyse our feelings and identify what we are feeling and why.

★   The first step is learning how to control our impulse to act.
★   The second step is feeling empathy for others which can hold back our anger or toxic attitude.
★   The third step is recognizing our tendency to use certain emotions in particular situations.
★   The fourth step is developing productive self-talk which can help us to stop our actions long enough for our thinking brain (*neocortex*) to thoroughly analyse the situation and make a rational decision. This will hold at bay the feeling brain (*amygdala*) which is the first impulse and alarm system of self-protection, until such time as needed.

2. Explicate

The best way to learn is by teaching. Being a leader yourself and taking action will help you use your emotional intelligence which encompasses self-motivation, self-control, managing emotions, recognizing the emotions in others, empathy and self-awareness. All are important factors in building and maintaining positive relationships. Developing EQ takes hard work and dedication to remain true to your own aspirations for personal development. In many offices there are employees who are unhappy and not able to deal with the stress resulting from the demands of organizations. This pressure causes problems in their personal lives which enter into the workplace. When we explicate we resolve, untangle, and unravel the day-to-day problems in our human interactions. By doing this we become the "change agents" of our own behaviour and thus we are part of the solution, rather than the problem. By coming to grips with the underlining issues of human interactions, we help others to manage their emotions through our emotional maturity and self-acceptance. When we teach or model EQ behaviour, we also learn. It is a time when we can utilize our inner skills to help others to plug in the gaps that exist between the relationships within the office.

Learning the art of effective EQ explication is a skill which can be cultivated by utilizing the following strategies:

(1) **Modelling EQ behaviour.** Becoming by doing is a useful technique for building the skills of self-empowerment. If we do not act as we wish to be we will never develop the habits of emotional intelligence. The ability to demonstrate productive behaviours that are based on beneficial feelings will increase our potential for meaningful interaction with other people. When we blend what we know with what we do, we build confidence and personal efficacy which results in self-motivation, self-esteem and perseverance when facing adversity. Modelling also provides others with a role model which is useful in a work setting.

If you are in a leadership role, this skill is vital for developing synergy and values throughout the organization. Even if you are not in a management position you can still become a model of EQ through your actions and genuine comfortableness with yourself and others.

(2) **Facilitating change.** Change agents are people who are proactive and are willing to make change within themselves first and then throughout the organization. They see the value of breaking down the barriers of complacency, hostility, and fear. When you think like a change agent you work toward personal and professional transformations which creates synergy and productivity. It is easy for us to say we are only one isolated person, so how can we change offices that are not positive? Maybe at first, you are unable to change your work environment but you can change how you view yourself, your potential, and your attitude. In every situation, it takes one person to begin the change process and one person to move toward building a better atmosphere. It is self-empowering to recognize that you can be happy and prosperous even when others try and put you down. It's in what you think and how you feel.

3.   Supplicate

This is to humbly ask for help and letting go of pride which blocks us from reaching out to other people. In business environments trust is usually missing and individuals do not feel comfortable with sharing a vulnerable spot which could hurt their professional position. In many cases, what limits trust is dishonesty in expressing real emotional concerns which become disguised as conceit, jealousy, and hidden fears. In order to strip away the layers of unproductive communication, we must be able to ask and seek help in developing better synergy and co-operation within our offices. This is the only way to add value to an office team and to discover the reasons for poor interactions and unproductive relationships. Learning the art of effective EQ supplication is a skill which can be cultivated by utilizing the following strategies:

(1) **Learning how to ask.** One of the problems with asking is not knowing how. In some work environments, competition and getting ahead can ruin team and peer relationships and are stumbling blocks to asking for help. However you can ask for help in ways that will not diminish your professionalism, nor jeopardize your career advancement. Four approaches to asking for help:

★ *Fact-finding mission.* This approach places you in control of leading a personal expedition of sorting through and finding out facts before making a decision on an action. This helps you maintain an appearance of understanding that more information is needed and that you know how to gather data appropriately.

★ *Respected authority seeker.* This approach puts you in a position of self-confidence in being able to acknowledge that someone else may be an authority and you respect their knowledge. Most people who are insecure can't accept that they are limited in some way and someone else has more information. This pride will undermine their development and prevent them from reaching out to others. In many cases you may even build better relationships when you respect your colleagues' abilities.

★ *Student position.* This approach places you in a position of learning and wanting to improve. Most people enjoy sharing knowledge when they are approached as a teacher. This should be done not as a primary school student but as a Harvard-type student who wishes to build on an already enormous bank of knowledge. Being a student does not mean you are lower or unintelligent. It means that you are seeking to learn more and to build upon your knowledge base. Remember that students can quickly become teachers if they take the time to listen and observe.

★ *Guide and partner.* This approach asks for guidance in finding the way to understand a particular issue or problem and offers an opportunity for a partner for successful resolution. This is a win/win strategy plan where the seeker of help and the provider team up to share in the rewards of the winning situation. This requires a carefully thought-out plan on how to establish a positive association while gathering the help needed.

(2) **Reciprocation.** One good deed deserves another. Often people forget when others have helped them by failing to return support or advice when appropriate. We have all experienced times when a request is just not possible to fill even though the person has been helpful in the past. Usually, if time is taken to explain the reasons for not responding it can eliminate bad feelings. Being labelled a user is not positive and can be hazardous when you need someone again. The old saying: "what goes around comes around" is true when failing to reciprocate when someone has helped you.

(3) **Openness.** This means being willing to receive and give assistance to colleagues and other people. Attitudes such as arrogance, egoism, and self-importance can close you off from others. In the long run this disposition can get people at a distance and it works poorly in team settings. Being bountiful and personally committed to others is a positive way to improve an office environment.

4. INVESTIGATE

This is when you seek to understand what are the fears, dreams, and major problems of your colleagues. This will help you to translate this information into an EQ perspective which is helpful in recognizing the emotions of others, having empathy, and improving relationships. A problem with this EQ skill is that people generally do not take the time to get to know the people they work with every day. Even customers go unnoticed until there is a problem. It is difficult to know how to relate to an individual until you know something about them.

When I was Vice-President of a charitable organization and responsible for raising US$6 million in one year, I remember a volunteer who was recruited to work in my department. She had a wonderful personality and understood the dynamics of fund-raising. However, whenever I assigned her to talk with business managers she would find an excuse not to show up or complete her task. I was being pressured to dismiss her and use another recruit. But I found her to be a sincere and wonderful person who was giving of her time because she cared. I sat down with her and conducted my own investigation in a non-threatening way. I began by asking her to tell me about herself and her professional life.

After spending some time with her I found that she was afraid of rejection by people she felt were better than her. This meant managers. She had been a bank-teller and never interacted with company executives other than to report to them. It was hard for her to imagine making a presentation in front of them. We discovered that her self-image and self-esteem were low when it came to people in high positions. Instead of letting her go, I cultivated her and let her come with me when I gave presentations to CEOs and other executives. I slowly integrated her into the discussion and after a while she felt confident to go on her own. She became one of my best fund-raisers. Without taking the time to investigate I wouldn't have discovered her problems nor would I have uncovered a solution. Investigation should be a routine process for building emotional intelligence in the workplace. It should be done in a non-threatening manner and for the betterment of the employees and the organization. Learning the art of effective EQ Investigation is a skill which can be cultivated by utilizing the following strategies:

(1) **Keep people's best interests in mind.** Uncovering information which can be helpful to building people up instead of tearing them down is a positive endeavour. Listening to gossip and one-sided perspectives is not productive. Although there are times when the negative information is true there may be other ways to help a person improve. Keeping the best interests of people in mind will help you to investigate with openness, fairness and empathy. This does not apply when there are morally inappropriate or unethical issues at hand. Most instances require understanding and the ability to seek the best way to help a colleague or customer.

(2) **Probe without judgement.** Finding information about a person should be done without a preconceived opinion in mind. People can quickly spot those who condemn them.

It is important to maintain an open and direct form of questioning which allows people to express what they are thinking and feeling. Giving individuals the benefit of the doubt is the best way to go until enough evidence shows another viewpoint is needed.

(3) **Take the time.** In a busy and competitive workplace, where technology and information is in abundance, it is easy to forget to be human and to care for one another. There must be time to find out how others are feeling and whether anyone is in need of help. You do not have to become a caseworker or psychologist, just a friendly and sincere, "how are you?" or "how did your meeting

go?". It will go a long way in becoming closer to the person you spend so much time with in the course of a week. Think how office life would change if everyone took the time to care.

(4) Build co-operation. Investigations should result in co-operation and building trust. Once you have discovered a personal or professional problem it is helpful to find a common ground for helping the individual work on the issue. If you find a colleague is afraid of speaking up for fear of being ridiculed, offer your support in helping them to speak up and know someone who will support them. Also, let them know that not everyone is likely to ridicule and encourage them to stand on their own.

(5) Be discreet and keep trust. Office gossip and failing to maintain a trust can destroy relationships. The ability to be discreet with information and knowing how to keep a trust are vital to building a better office environment. I have seen offices become battlefields when people start acting unprofessionally and talking about other people's personal affairs. The office shouldn't be the official place for dealing with personal matters. However, it is a place where people interact daily and it is hard to separate personal and professional lives. It can be impossible in some settings. Therefore, it is imperative that peers learn to manage information delicately and set a standard where gossip and inappropriate information is not welcomed.

5. MOTIVATE

In the builder's concept of EQ in the workplace, there is a need to motivate yourself as well as others. It is said that negative attitudes are catching and positive attitudes are contagious. An office filled with optimism, joint enthusiasm, and team spirit will do more for an individual's personal and professional morale than any other reward. The feeling of belonging to an office that works together and empowers each other is a powerful one. How you can catch the fever of motivation is to motivate. Think of when you play with a baby. You begin by trying to motivate him to laugh and feel happy. You smile and make funny gestures. Most times it works and sometimes it doesn't, depending on the baby, but you do it again until it catches on. The same should be true in the office. We must motivate one another. By doing so we increase our own motivation. People are not babies but they are human beings who need to feel valued. Taking the time to become an optimist, an enthusiast, and a team player will inject a wondrous synergy. It takes time to catch on but when you are not there you will be missed. In time, others will rise to the opportunity to bring sunshine instead of gloom while the "nay" sayers will hold back progress at the office. Remember that stopping a negative cycle begins with one person. Others will follow. Learning the art of effective EQ motivation is a skill which can be cultivated by utilizing the following strategies:

(1)   **Being proactive.** Instead of reacting to negative situations, start a new trend by being proactive and begin a new cycle of excitement and esteem for your work. Take the initiative to create reasons to be positive and enlist the help of willing colleagues. Do not let others determine your disposition and spoil your mood. Take charge and give them an opportunity to follow your lead. Have faith in your ability to spread positive emotions and challenge others to join in.

(2)   **Being a visionary.** If you do not see the worth or value in your organization it is difficult to be motivated. You must create a vision of how you can become a better employee even when the environment might not welcome you. This will give you focus on

what can be and will move you in a positive direction rather than stagnating in a negative and uncooperative place. I have used this technique personally when faced with uncooperative staff in work situations. This helped me keep the faith while working through my challenges. As a result, the customers noticed me and I built a wonderful support base which was helpful to me.

(3) **Developing a specific plan.** If you are a manager or a person who must manage themselves in a difficult work environment, it is productive to develop a plan of action of how you will handle yourself and cultivate the support needed to make positive changes within your organization. If change is not feasible, develop a plan for how you can accomplish your goals, and either triumph in your current situation or find a better path. This plan should include, but is not limited to the following:

★ What is your goal?
★ What is your current situation (both positive and negative)?
★ Who are your allies and what are your challenges?
★ What steps will it take to reach your goal?
★ What is your time frame?
★ What is Plan B when this plan needs to change?
★ How will you deal with your challenges and setbacks?

Re-building our inner wall takes the three Cs:

Concentration
Commitment
Care

Without a builder's concept or attention to the five skill areas of demonstration, explication, supplication, investigation, and motivation we will wander aimlessly trying to figure out why we are not achieving personal or professional satisfaction. We may spend years working next to people we hardly know or care about in an office environment where everyone is waiting for someone else to take the lead to change. Building EQ starts and ends with you. All of the books and seminars will not unlock the door to your inner wall unless you allow it and embrace the wonders of what you can develop inside. Managing our emotions and dealing with people from the heart as well as the mind is the best way to start improving our work-life. It provides long-lasting results and positive direction toward building bridges necessary for productivity and profitability.

PART TWO

EQ DYNAMICS IN THE WORKPLACE

EQ Dynamics in the Workplace

There are many dynamics operating in the workplace today. We read and hear about several of them daily. Yet the most pervasive and highly hidden driving force to human development and workplace success receives little or no attention. This little known indicator of how we excel in life and the important role it plays in our social and career success is called "emotional intelligence". The level of our emotional intelligence can be the underlying cause of success or part of the problem facing businesses today. I spend many hours explaining the term to business managers and the need to understand our emotional make-up in order to harness those sabotaging feelings and behaviours which diminish personal and professional progress. In most cases, I am asked how does this seemingly "soft" issue impact on the bottom line of profit and productivity.

EQ can be the determinant of how successful or unsuccessful a company is. External signs that EQ is missing in organizations are when for example:

1. Store clerks leave customers unattended while they talk with fellow workers until customers have to ask for help
2. Bank tellers are unable or unwilling to address customers concerns
3. Financial wizards become irritated because customers ask questions which they think are stupid and answer in a way that would insult the customers' IQ level. Customers then leave, vowing to find another investment opportunity.

Internal signs that EQ is missing in organizations are when, for example:

1. Colleagues are uncooperative in helping one another
2. Managers lose their tempers and tell subordinates off because they ask for long-needed breaks
3. Colleagues refuse to see the hard work of their peers, criticizing only their mistakes
4. Colleagues trust one another with information only to find out they have been betrayed
5. Depression and boredom are present
6. Employees undermine one another's efforts

Experiences like these, all speak to the problems of not managing our emotions, a lack of empathy and consideration, or not being attuned to the needs of others. These core issues are fundamental to building teams, improving morale, increasing productivity, and empowering staff to function more proactively. It is also needed in peer relationships, customer service, and creating win/win situations. Without the loyalty and co-operation of employees the office environment will not be a harmonious place where respect and honest interaction can take place. Instead it will become a battleground like many offices today find themselves fighting in.

Why Create an EQ Architectural Design?

An EQ Architectural Design involves enhancing an organization from the ground. One aspect of doing this is to understand the importance of the emotional life of people within their organizations; whether they are managers, employees, customers, shareholders, suppliers, or other professionals important to the prosperity of a business. Each of these groups has a function and relationship which is tied to the level of profit of an organization. But more importantly and often misunderstood is that all of these people have one thing in common: they have a mind and a heart which is made up of emotions, habits, experiences, and behaviours. To deny this fact would be to ignore their humanness.

Mismanagement of relationships stems from two levels: not being aware of ourselves and not being aware of other people. Business should be synonymous with emotional attunement. In successful transactions, mergers, joint ventures, and other business investment opportunities people must be able to harmonize with one another. If not, the business opportunity becomes a liability.

A wealthy man I knew seemed to make money, but went from one business deal to the next, leaving a trail of angry and disgruntled employees and partners. His business ethics were questionable and he wasn't able to achieve the right mix of acumen and tact. He usually knew how to make the deal profitable for himself, but he didn't know how to make people happy. His approach lacked empathy and concern for others and he never noticed how his words turned people off. I observed him in a meeting that started out positive and he single-handedly turned it into a fight. His lack of self-awareness and inability to recognize the emotions in others limited his success. He made some money but had no friends to share it with. This left him restless and searching for real meaning in his life.

How do we begin to make change in the place where we spend so much time and which we depend on for our livelihoods? First, by changing ourselves. Second, by really seeing and caring about the people whom we see every day. To care means to want to get to know our peers and to develop relationships which are co-empowering and helpful in accomplishing corporate goals. What is needed in offices is more "brilliancy". In this context this means to shine and radiate. People who have brilliancy are the jewels of an organization. You do not need to have an abundance of charisma, physical looks, or a winning outgoing personality to have brilliancy. This is an inner quality which is matched by your insight into understanding and knowing people and being able to attune your emotions to theirs, while maintaining your own self-confidence. This creates the glow of brilliancy. To others, it is not necessarily something that is seen, it is felt. You know when you have met a terrific person. It leaves you feeling better and empowered. Adding brilliancy in our work environment can start with you.

Eleven Secrets to Building Peer and Customer Relations

It all begins and ends with the core of the matter: the heart.

To begin building peer and customer relations, requires knowing ten secrets.

Secret 1:
Most People are Just as Afraid of Not Succeeding as You Are

It is beneficial to avoid using self-defeating and toxic behaviours to cover up low self-image and self-esteem. Determining where you have learned to judge yourself or others so harshly and recognizing the need to change your way of feeling will uncover a new way of dealing with your self-defeating paradigm. Try and understand what emotions trigger a fear of failure and how you may be using these feelings to hold others back.

SECRET 2:
CUSTOMERS DO NOT NEED YOU

You need them. The best way for you to grow as a professional is to understand and deal with customers from a positive, emotional level. This means recognizing and responding to how they feel, treating them as valuable people and seeking to honestly help them. Attuning yourself to their needs rather than your own will give you the wisdom to deal with conflict and confrontation when a customer is displeased. You will also learn how to concentrate on what will make them happy rather than on what they should have done to consider your feelings. When spending money customers are not interested in dealing with your emotions they are interested in you dealing with theirs.

SECRET 3:
WHAT YOU SAY TO YOURSELF MAKES A DIFFERENCE IN HOW YOU REACT TO PUT-DOWNS FROM OTHERS

Our self-talk can be a friend or foe, it all depends on whether we receive negative or positive messages about what was said to us. I recall a very bright and articulate woman who did not know this secret. She would internalize put-downs as direct attacks against her character. At times she was correct in recognizing that an insensitive person was attacking her character and not what she did. However, she made the mistake of believing what others said about her even when their remarks were unfair and unproductive. As a result she felt unworthy and it affected her career success. She was overlooked for promotions because she kept telling herself that she was incapable of achieving at a higher level. Learning to use our self-talk to our benefit is an EQ skill worth cultivating. Putting into our brain positive and realistic messages is stimulating and uplifting and should replace self-defeating and pessimistic thoughts.

SECRET 4:
IMPULSE CONTROL IS AT THE CORE OF EMOTIONAL INTELLIGENCE

Learning to control our impulses is fundamental to emotional maturity and success. Our neural circuitry systems in the brain are programmed to call us to action. This prehistoric trait is a hard one to forego. In an advanced civilization where diplomacy and thought is now vital to success, it is imperative that we save the old disposition of either fighting or fleeing for times of potential bodily harm. It is wise to develop the skill of stifling the urge to act until you have the appropriate information to make the right response. In many cases of interpersonal interactions, it is best to control the urge to demonstrate anger, disgust and other self-defeating emotions unless you have perfected the art of expressing your feelings in a most appropriate and highly professional manner.

SECRET 5:
UNDERSTANDING THE IMPACT YOUR WORDS OR ACTIONS HAVE ON OTHERS IS A KEY FACTOR IN EQ SUCCESS

The Stormin' Norman's of the world who bluntly and without thought to how others feel, tell it how they think it is, can find themselves leaving people angry, frustrated and unmotivated. Thinking through how others may feel about the information you have to share and spending time finding the best way to communicate with others will avoid inhumane situations. Sometimes it is unavoidable not to hurt someone's feelings. But if you recognize this will happen and offer support and a way for them to maintain their dignity you will have demonstrated EQ caring and consideration. The saying "it's not what you say but how you say it" is partly true. A better way to express the saying would be: "it is what you say and how you say it that makes all the difference."

SECRET 6:
YOU CAN'T MANAGE OTHERS UNTIL YOU CAN MANAGE YOURSELF

The first rule a manager or leader should learn is to manage themselves. This means learning to self-regulate emotions and actions. There is nothing more disconcerting than to have a leader preaching a sermon he does not live by.

An outgoing and ambitious business executive was responsible for 50 employees in an up and coming manufacturing company. He lived to talk and fancied himself as an old-time preacher. He would constantly remind people of the importance of learning to take life less seriously and to laugh more. His famous saying was: "let your ego go on vacation while at work". He enjoyed spreading humour and thought this lightened the workload. The problem was he used this approach to avoid serious discussions with his employees. When someone raised the issue of overtime pay he would laugh it off, or when another employee would complain about the poor lunch-room facilities he joked that his salary could be used as a donation to renovate the lunch-room. For the most part, employees genuinely wanted to like him and many found him to be good-natured. At the annual company dinner, the Chairman of the Board made a joke about his business executive's stinginess and said that his month's pay would be auctioned on a first-come first-served basis. The crowd went wild with laughter. Everyone except the business executive. He sat there red-faced and unable to control his anger. When it was his turn, his anger won through and the language he used would have been edited by any upstanding television station. The audience was stunned. He lost his credibility that evening and his humour at work was never the same. Employees boldly expressed anger at their work responsibilities and conditions. Dissension arose and changed the heart of the company. Employees stopped carrying the load. After a couple of years and many battles, the business executive quietly retired. This example shows that it is not only important to manage our emotions but to also show empathy for our employees. Often their concerns are legitimate and should be addressed.

SECRET 7:
IT IS NOT GOOD TO VENT ANGER

Well-intended advice has said that it is good to vent anger as a way of getting it out of your system. This is not true. Venting actually expands the emotion throughout your system and heightens the stimulus to act in ways that can be unproductive. A better way to deal with anger is to:

- recognize that you are angry
- know your limits
- get away from the object of your anger to allow yourself time to cool off
- do something that diverts your attention away from your concern
- look at the situation from the other person's perspective

I remember learning that a colleague of mine was saying nasty things about me behind my back. I didn't appreciate his remarks but decided it wasn't worth a confrontation. One day I needed to speak with him about a project we were working on. I called him at least four times but he never returned my calls. My employee informed me that he had just received a call from the colleague I was trying to reach telling him that he couldn't return my calls because he was too busy. I felt my blood pressure shoot up and my adrenaline level escalate. I felt like grabbing the telephone and shouting at him. Being that it was at the end of the day, I instead decided to go for a walk. I said a prayer asking for release of this emotion and asked myself: "why am I really angry?"

What I discovered was that my ego was in the way and I wanted him to respect me. Why was that necessary?

The fact that I knew he didn't like me made him more important than he should have been. My desire to please people surfaced and when I couldn't get him to like me, I became angry by his slight. I released the anger and found that his childish antics no longer affected me. Had I kept venting it, the anger would have surfaced everything bad he had ever said and done to me. In fact, I would have invented more just to give fuel to my anger. Through this process I found that his approval was no longer important and got the information I needed from another source.

Secret 8:
Competition and Co-operation are Compatible

So often we see the world as one big competitive place where getting ahead means someone has to step back or lose. This mentality perpetuates a "me only" attitude which allows room for only one winner. This philosophy is negative in all human situations. Accomplishing at the detriment of others never builds support and is quickly challenged. A competitive spirit is important in acquiring success, but when it represents the cornerstone of how we relate to other people it then becomes destructive. Co-operation is knowing that winning is important, but also appreciating the value of building alliances and creating partnerships which have a longer sustaining element, than riding as a lone ranger.

SECRET 9:
OUR CHARACTER SPEAKS LOUDER THAN WORDS

Who we are is often overshadowed by what we say and do. If we do not care about people and find love to be a boring and useless emotion, our character will house a core that holds people in disdain and mistrust, Even when our outer appearance generates a positive attitude. In time people will see the discrepancy and the true meaning behind the phoniness. Manipulation is a skill some people have cultivated extremely well. They use it at whim and are calculating. This kind of deception can only last for a period of time and demands that the person be cunning and cover their tracks. The stress and anxiety of being found out adds to the drama that unfolds in their daily lives and makes people around them live and work in difficult situations.

Betty was a woman with an external appearance of warmth and kindness but a heart of stone. She built layers of anger over hurt to shield her from pain. In her professional life, dissension and mistrust abounded. As time went by people noticed that her smile was false and what she said was inconsistent with what she did. Progressively, her hidden agenda came to light as her true character emerged, and her actions began to unravel the layers she had so carefully created.

SECRET 10:
SELF-MOTIVATION AND PERSISTENCE COME FROM KNOWING HOW TO DIRECT OUR EMOTIONS

Often we look for others to motivate us and provide the stimulus to achieve. When we are young our parents usually provide us with the encouragement and guidance to realize our goals. As we grow older this motivation is derived from what we hope to have someday and the demands of maintaining a job. These are all temporary and often superficial stimulants. The underlining source of motivation comes from within. Self-motivation is the internal drive and will to overcome obstacles and to keep moving forward when disappointment and frustration occur. Self-motivation is the best gift you can give yourself in times of difficulty and even when feeling complacent. It allows you to be proactive in taking control over how you feel and over your actions. Athletes know best how important self-motivation is to their sport. Self-motivation is a necessary component to building positive and productive customer service.

Increasing the level of our service as professionals includes developing four key aspects of our internal make-up:

(1) **Temperament.** We all have a temperament which we are born with. Our moods and disposition dictates how we deal with people, situations, and demands. Some people are very low-key and slow to become angry while other people are more volatile and less able to handle pressure. Our dispositions can be detected when we are babies. My brother rarely cried and would play quietly, in contrast to me. I was always crying and seeking attention from my mother. The good news is that we can change our temperament. It is not something that we must live with for the rest of our lives. We can choose to be more patient or kinder or even more co-operative. The will is there when we honestly decide to use it. Dealing with customers or peers in an office requires an assessment of how we deal with our emotions and our moods. Two ways to do this is to separate our temperament into two categories:

★ *Hot spots.* We consciously know what and who makes us uncomfortable, angry, defensive, insecure, frustrated or depressed. Recognizing what triggers certain emotions will help us develop our self-talk and mindset to create a mechanism to protect us from self-expression that may be harmful to us and others. Instead of going straight to an emotional hijacking—where we lose control by bypassing our thinking brain and going straight to our limbic brain which signals an emergency and calls for action, we can use different approaches such as: visualization, disassociation, empathy, or removing ourselves physically at soon as possible. As we face situations which trigger a learned habit of response, we can interject self-talk for a more proper way of responding. Such self-talk could be: "Stop, this is not worth the anger, I am a person of strength and influence, I can deal with this matter." This will influence us away from our normal tendency to react inappropriately.

★ *Readiness Process.* This is planning in advance how you would react to situations, people or scenarios even when there is no real knowledge of such things occurring. This will imprint in your mind a suggestion as to what to do if, and when, you are faced with a difficult emotional position. The real challenge is to use this readiness process when emotions get involved. It takes practice and self-awareness to work on this process and use it effectively. The process includes:

→ identifying the immediate emotion and the corresponding hot spot with the underlining cause
→ using another approach than one you would normally (if unproductive)
→ focusing on a positive outcome
→ finding a reason to empathize
→ using self-talk to encourage you to rise upon the temptation to lash out and employ old self-defeating tendencies

It may seem like a long and laborious process but it only takes a second to implement when practised.

(2) **Hope.** Without desire there is no real drive to achieve. We must want to provide excellent service and create a personality that is hopeful, humble, and assertive in making sure that the customer is receiving our best. Hope comes in several dimensions, for example, some people hope that:

Unproductive Relationship Dimension

- a customer will not ask them to provide service
- others will fail
- others will be entrapped into disapproving positions
- dissension will prevail and harmony will be lost
- they will win at any cost and without any virtue

Negative Self-Paradigm Dimension

- they will fail (self-fulfilling prophecy)
- complacency (taking the easy way out)
- their workday ends quickly
- the business fails and they have a legitimate excuse for leaving
- they will not have to change or try new and innovative things

---

Positive and Productive Dimension

- the best in people and situations will occur

- others will win
- truth will prevail
- honesty will be pervasive
- they are providing five star quality service
- their actions are appropriate

Which category do you find yourself in most of the time? Hope is a pre-condition to "Optimism".

(3) **Optimism**. Without hope the chances of optimism are diminished. Optimism is the expectation and trust that things will work out for the best. It is the feeling deep down that we have the ability to accomplish and even triumph against the odds. Most successful people have a sense of optimism which keeps them grounded and progressive even when others discourage their efforts. Optimism gives you the inner strength to stay motivated and to stand apart from the crowd when your principles are being challenged. Optimism is an attitude which is manifested by a deep conviction and belief in the course you are taking.

Adequate planning, preparation and realistic projections are important to steering optimism in the right direction. The enemy of optimism is pessimism. A pessimist sees the world from the level of "I can't … It won't work because … In the past it didn't … life is bad … people are bad …" They see a cup half-empty, not half-full. This mentality robs people of the freedom to explore and see the potential in life. The pessimist usually drains the energy and positive spirit right out of an organization. Haven't you noticed certain individuals who whenever they walk into the room people begin to leave? These individuals seem to carry a gloom and doom attitude which makes everyone around them depressed. Certain individuals make themselves miserable with a self-defeatist attitude while other pessimists appear to thrive on their misery. They relish their struggles and the ability to complain instead of facing up to a challenge in a positive way. Haven't you seen a person who is upset and when someone tries to cheer them up they become angry with them? They prefer to stay miserable but most of all they want company to share in their misery. This destroys self-motivation and undermines personal and professional relationships.

(4) **Self-efficacy.** In self-motivation we must recognize and embrace our capacity to make things happen. The person who doesn't realize the importance of taking the first step in mending relationships or reaching out to other people will always be waiting for someone else to make the first move. The more inclined we are to take action and resolve conflicts, the better able we are to create a more productive working environment.

A friend of mine stayed angry with another mutual friend (who we will call Sally) for almost two years because Sally had not called her when she had promised and it resulted in my friend losing out on a potential business deal. My friend refused to call Sally to find out what happened. Sally in turn was angry because she had assumed that my friend didn't care about her or the business opportunity. This may seem like a petty reason for stopping an otherwise wonderful friendship—it was. This kind of misunderstanding comes directly from people not wanting to be the first to seek clarification, give apologies, or try and build relationships. Our pride and ego can get in the way of our reasoning and prevent us from giving and receiving love. This kind of attitude undermines interaction and creates bad feelings that can last too long. In the office setting, when peers miscommunicate there is a tendency to make assumptions which lead to negative attitudes and result in poor team work, *anomie* (lack of accepted norms, values and behaviours), heighten gossip and lower productivity.

We can achieve many of the things we set out to do. There will be times when we are unable to do everything exactly the way we have planned. But for the most part, we can produce our strongest desire with the four P's:

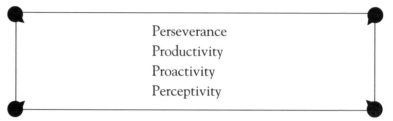

Perseverance
Productivity
Proactivity
Perceptivity

An exciting challenge for all of us is to empower ourselves to use the determination, self-esteem, and emotional intelligence to harness the potential we have and to use appropriate resources to recognize an opportunity. To seize an opportunity encompasses self-motivation and its sub-parts of temperament, hope, optimism, and self-efficacy along with preparation, skill development, focus, and effective research. A self-liberating notion is that we don't have to wait for the challenge to take hold of us, we can take hold of it.

No man or woman is an island, in and of, him or herself. It takes the collective support and collaboration of other people to help us reach our goals. Teams and departments working together can build a synergetic environment or a dismal existence. When people blend their self-efficacy and self-motivation together in harmony, the impact is wondrous to customers.

The future of our companies and the potential for our success depends on our efficacy in developing personal and professional inner power. This includes harnessing our capability, knowledge capacity and the depth of our hearts to deal with people in a caring and professional manner. The combination of our rational mind and emotional competence is at the heart of self-efficacy.

SECRET 11:
FROM SUCCESS TO SIGNIFICANCE

Wherever you are in life financially, spiritually, career or relationship-wise, the road should be heading in one direction: from success to significance. This means basically that success is defined by what you accomplish bringing self-fulfilment, reward, loving relationships, and work that means something to you and others. The end product is the significance of all your efforts in making a difference for other people. Significance not only to your family and friends, but to life itself. It is the way in which you have given of yourself in order to give meaning to people who you don't really know, yet have been influenced by you. Significance is shown by what you have done to make your environment a better place and how you have stood in the gap between what is good and what is bad. The ultimate is helping to build a bridge so that people can find their way back to what is positive and productive. This may sound like a tall order but it isn't at all when you think of the gifts that we have and the importance of remembering the little gestures in life. These gestures can be as simple as helping a colleague to solve a problem, praising someone who rarely receives a kind word, being sensitive to the needs of others, or working to rid your organization of toxic and sabotaging behaviours. It is building a place where people can have hope and optimism that you and the organization cares. Significance starts with valuing others as well as yourself.

The following is a true story. In Paris, 1912, a father won the honour of representing his country in the Olympics. His wife was scheduled to deliver their first baby, a boy, at the same time as the Olympics. Recognizing the importance of the birth of his son, he decided not to fulfil his lifelong dream of competing in the Olympic Games. Instead he chose to be present for the birth of his child. He never regretted the decision and never mentioned it to his son. Some twenty years later almost to the day, he received a letter from his son who wrote, "thanks for being there when I was born, I want you to have this special token of my deep love and respect for you." It was the gold medal the son had won in the Olympics of that year for the same sporting event his father gave up for his arrival in the world. The father was overwhelmed. The significance of the love between the father and his son went beyond any success in life.

Obstacles to Building EQ

1. Unhealthy Feelings and Actions

Fear, bias, jealousy, manipulation, intimidation, phoniness, and self-hate are a few of the words that can provide real obstacles to building EQ when brought to life by our minds and actions. Individuals who exhibit these attitudes and behaviours live in a whirlwind of internal conflict and suffering. We cannot deny that these negative feelings cast invisible shadows over our lives and often materialize into devious actions and hurtful words which dim our character and personality. Not only do these obstacles cause pain to others, they also diminish the bank of self-esteem we have inside which loses important chips every time we generate these behaviours which hurt ourselves as well as others.

2. Destructive Mindsets in Relationships

Another EQ obstacle is a destructive mindset. This happens when we strive to reach an ideal in order to be accepted by others which may be in conflict with who we really are. This serves as a root to many of our self-esteem problems. Traditionally, men are taught to compete and prove their prowess or success by what they win. Traditionally, women are taught to try to be the prettiest, nicest, and smartest as long as they do not turn their man off. In some cases women compete with other women by judging themselves by what the other woman has in relation to them. ...Is she prettier, better-dressed, does she have nicer hair... are the questions we often ask ourselves. All outward symbols of status and appeal.

Some men focus on what others have as a means of gaining success, but tend not to focus as much on appearance as women. For the most part, men use power as a means of controlling and holding onto a position of status which has been reserved for them because of their gender association. This mindset becomes a problem when they must work for, or with, women. What complicates relationships further is the difficult time some men have in communicating their feelings. The more threatened they feel the less they talk. Instead of expression, they use intimidation, and a commanding nature to diminish an individual's authority. Consequently this leaves these men feeling lonely, tense, and unable to enjoy casual friendships.

Women tend to project their unhappiness with themselves by being jealous of others, and feeling powerless when competing with men. Some women and even men, tend to vent their envy by trying to lower the esteem of others. This is done through gossip, inappropriate actions, and verbal and non-verbal means that intend to lower a person's confidence and potential. The messages we receive can be overt like women seeing themselves as competing with other women for the title of who is "the fairest of them all," or men seeing images of toughness and success (meaning to win at all cost) as a way of proving their worth. These attitudes toward gender roles are changing through progressive equality movements, but are still prevalent in many societies and must be continually addressed.

3. CONSpiRACy

A few years ago, when my husband was working for a big multinational company, we were attending a company party for the employees and their spouses. I was amused at how similar the setting was to a high school dance. The men gathered together in one corner and the women clustered in another. I noticed two women I knew who were looking my way and giggling. One of the women was the boss' wife. They had decided from previous encounters that I would not have entry into their unofficial corporate wives club because I did not fit their criteria which included: being a corporate-grown wife and not a career woman, being non-threatening (to women who did not recognize their own self-worth), and above all following the rules of the boss's wife. She usually passed judgement according to how threatened she was of you. If she wasn't threatened then you were in. If she was you were out. Another major requirement was that you were to acknowledge her as the indisputable leader. When it became obvious I would not be invited into her elite club, it brought to mind how many of us seem not to fit into any category or group where people want to dominate others. As unique individuals, we should stand on our own and not settle for friendships that depend upon a status symbol. Rather we must seek to establish real and valuable relationships that are empowering, fulfilling, and supportive of others.

As the party got under way, I could tell the two women were "weaving a plot", of which I would be the main character. As I predicted, the show was about to start. The follower of the boss' wife went over to my husband and flirted loudly with exaggerated motion and dialogue. The room grew quiet as people watched the show in amazement. I appeared cool although the room's temperature, or my own, was becoming somewhat off the normal range. As I laughed and talked with our friends, the follower became very dissatisfied that her actions were not getting the proper response from me. She decided to draw me into her performance by making me a co-star. She called my name and proceeded to tell me how handsome my husband was, and how lucky I was to have him and to caution me that if I wasn't careful someone would steal him away. My poor husband was in shock at this outward display of boldness and if a trap door had been available, he would have gone through it. I turned, smiled, faced her squarely and said with enthusiasm, "he certainly is terrific and I believe your announcement deserves a round of applause." Everyone started clapping and laughing. I made her the butt of the scene rather than the reverse as she had planned. Meanwhile her friend was standing with a perfect view to observe if their plan to make me jealous had worked. To their disappointment it had not.

We sometimes resort to childish behaviour as examplified above. This only undermines us as women and makes our inclusion in the workforce and within the social structures it mandates more difficult and frustrating. We should work in supporting one another and build coalitions as men have done for years. We have come a long way, but we still have miles to travel before we can rid ourselves of envy which manifests itself into demeaning behaviours.

4. INSECURITY AND THREAT

When men feel threatened they can use means such as intimidation, power playing, or using unfair demands in the work environment to quell this threat.

A male boss who held a high position in a corporation was fearful of a younger executive. To maintain an edge he would keep his subordinate waiting for pertinent information and purposely set meeting dates sometimes at 6:30 in the morning, and then not show up. This disrespect and unpredictable behaviour made the young executive feel insecure. The boss would hastily call and ask for information and when the young executive returned an elaborate and well-prepared work, his boss would return the original document with one misspelled work circled in red and no other comments. He totally disregarded the outstanding report but chose instead to focus on the one mistake. The boss used intimidation and power to undermine and lower the enthusiasm and potential of his employee by diminishing his confidence.

Too often these tactics are used on women with an added dimension of sexual harassment which now men are finding in the workplace as well. It takes self-confidence, determination, and political astuteness to deal with these "power hoarders" (people who use position and authority to purposely break the confidence, career potential, and self-respect of the employees they find threatening).

Ways to deal with bosses or peers who try to break your spirit and emotional balance are:

- Avoid giving them your power by believing you are not effective or capable.
- Keep a home diary of each discussion just in case you need it at evaluation time.
- Excel in your work and build bridges with other co-workers.
- Maintain a paper trail where you document your actions and your work while keeping an up-to-date file.
- Always be consistent, pleasant, and professional with all employees including your boss.
- Keep your problems with your boss to yourself unless you are sharing the information with a trusted colleague or mentor.
- Attempt to establish a co-operative relationship with your boss by giving sincere compliments, asking for ways to improve, and sharing some of your concerns about your working conditions. Do not present it as a gripe.
- Keep looking for other opportunities if your situation does not improve.

5. Jealousy

People who are jealous of our talents in reality feel inferior and will often try to convince us we are not worthy and our gifts not that valuable.

A teacher I know told me of a story involving a friend of his who was jealous of his PhD degree which he had earned while maintaining a full-time teaching position. His friend, who held a high school degree, upon learning of his achievement, commented that getting a PhD degree was not that hard, nor did you need to be very smart to receive one. The question was if it is so easy why hadn't he gained his? This individual and others spend a lifetime trying to diminish the efforts of others in an attempt to place themselves higher. Some people can be very tricky in their quest to put obstacles in our way and decrease our personal power in an attempt to enhance their own.

I recall a man who kept asking me, as if he were an authority and a judge, what credentials I had to write a book. He proceeded to interrogate me on the principles I was using to write and why it was taking me so long to finish—after having written for only three months. It wasn't the questions that were offensive, but the manner and superior way in which he asked them, especially since he had never written anything similar. His underlying attitude and condescending air was intended to decrease my enthusiasm and confidence, making me doubt my own abilities. What he didn't realize, however, was he was actually giving me an example to use in my book!

6. Gossip

Many people like to spread gossip. I have heard people justify this by saying this is only human nature. What happens when we entertain this kind of petty exploitation of another person's life and problems is that we avoid looking in the mirror and do not deal with the problems we create, or are the recipient of. To participate in gossip results in a waste of time and does nothing to increase our potential. When taken too far it will decrease it. There is a difference between receiving information which may be useful to you and receiving information that is intended to hurt or destroy a person's reputation. Gossip of any kind is destructive and unproductive. It makes an environment a hostile and uncomfortable place to work in and should not be tolerated.

7. Subliminal Negative Conditioning

Subliminal negative conditioning happens all around us and can get into our psyche if we are not conscious of it. Even in school, when rules for behaviour are presented, a detailed overview of what will happen if we are bad overshadows any mention of the rewards to be gained if we are good. Television highlights the negative to a greater degree than the positive. For example, how many happy, well-adjusted people do we see on talk shows? Or how many of the role models we look up to have lives that are enriching to themselves or to other people? Unfortunately not that many. The people we look up to in the entertainment industry have just as many or more problems as we do. Yet many of us espouse to emulate them. I wonder how many of the stars we envy would like to trade places with ordinary and sensible people? When I mentioned to a friend that so many talk shows deal with unhappy or neurotic personalities, her comment was, "the ratings would go down and people would stop watching the programs if positive issues were the major focus." This illustrated further that we are conditioned not only to expect the negative, but also to ask for it.

8. Not Letting Go

Even people with high self-esteem and emotional intelligence will become depressed and sometimes disillusioned when faced with disappointments in life. It is difficult to face personal turmoil in relationships, family crises and career setbacks without at times becoming discouraged or angry. Feeling depressed for a period of time is normal and can be cleansing.

However, it is important to express feelings and not keep them inside, or pretend they don't exist. Allowing ourselves to feel the pain and work through it is positive. The problem sets in when we can't or won't release it, thus not allowing ourselves to move on. With every adversity, disappointment, and hardship comes an opportunity for growth and self-improvement. A failure, whether personal or professional, can turn into a positive experience if we make a conscious effort to be creative in our thinking and analyse ways we can learn from the adversity rather than giving into it.

One important difference between individuals who achieve personal success in life from those who do not is that they have drawn upon their internal skills to help them through difficult times. They are not overly critical of themselves, or bitter toward the person who caused adversity in their lives. When we believe ourselves to be worthy and valuable, we allow ourselves to feel hurt and depressed about a situation, but we also give ourselves permission to move on with optimism and self-respect. We can feel a sense of liberation when we combine our emotional side with our thinking side to help create a balance in our perspectives. This will provide a leverage against depression so that it won't consume us.

Six Rules of EQ Success

Everything in life has its meaning and instruction for how to cultivate and realize success. Some people call it codes, others call it requirements, or process. But whatever word is used, it is important to create guidelines or rules as you venture toward achieving any form of personal growth. Emotional Intelligence advocates certain ground rules before moving into the work of developing the cognitive, emotional, and behaviour skills important to managing ourselves more effectively. These rules give us a benchmark for assessing our progress.

Rule 1:
There are More Ways to be Smart Than Through Intellect

Knowing how to deal with people, having interpersonal skills, and the ability to resolve conflicts harmoniously are important ways of being smart. In leadership or any human interaction, the smarter we are in EQ, the better chance we have in accomplishing our goals, making meaningful friendships, and being happy.

Rule 2:
Your EQ is More Important Than Your IQ Because it is What Determines Your Success in Life

Skill, intellect and knowledge are important in a highly technological and information-driven global marketplace. However, intelligence without empathy or awareness of ourselves and other people makes us similar to a computer—facts without emotion. Human beings are more sensitive and require more connectedness than just data processing and retrieval. This calls for people to be attuned to the needs of individuals as well as themselves. Customers care about quality products but are just as interested or even more so in the way they are treated. Insincere, thoughtless, smug and uncooperative employees, no matter how brilliant, will not make a sale if their EQ is not as high or higher than their IQ.

Rule 3:
IQ is Unchangeable but EQ can Change for the Better

The exciting news is that although our IQ is established from birth and is unchangeable, our level of EQ is not destiny. We can grow and develop the skills and attitudes to take us far in life. Many successful people do not necessarily have high IQs. What they do have is the ability to relate effectively with people, and to deal with life's challenges constructively and effectively.

Self-motivation is a key to success and is a vital tool when trying to overcome many obstacles. People with high EQ have the will and desire to make it in their personal and professional worlds. The fact that we can reprogram our brain and learn new habits should be encouraging.

We don't have to live with self-sabotaging emotions and behaviours. We can be proactive and seek professional help in sorting through intense emotional conflicts. But for less intense emotional problems we can work on them ourselves and with the help of trusted family members, friends, and colleagues. Everyone has aspects of their personal make-up that needs improving. No one is perfect.

Rule 4:
Self-Understanding and a Desire for Personal Growth is a First Step Toward Developing EQ

Before we can embark on a personal development program or any course for change we must have a sense of who we are, what we think, and how we feel. We have to be able to recognize and identify our emotions and understand the cause of our feelings in order to deal with them effectively. It's like wanting to buy a dress but being in a supermarket. It will not be possible unless that store sells dresses.

(1) **Get to the right store** or the right place of knowing where you are emotionally.

(2) **Have the desire to want to do things better.** Often we wish to change, for example, lose weight, but we never leave our sofas or attempt to change. Change means action. Getting up and doing. Our desire focuses our mind toward the end result.

(3) **Develop a plan,** determine the resources needed, chart a course of action, take action, monitor progress, and practise.

Rule 5:
Emotions Have Intelligence

Throughout many of our experiences we were told that emotions were something soft and unreasonable and that they had no real significance in our quest for knowledge. Emotions were even viewed as unproductive and should not have a place in the business world. This couldn't be further from the truth. Emotions are at the centre of the workplace and can be the reason for failure or success in many business endeavours.

Ethics, values, vision, and mission are all terms which have an underpinning of emotions involved. Too often employees view these signs as empty gestures by management because they lack the reality of what is happening in many business environments. The corporate statement of intent does not match what is practised.

Intent and motive are symbolic when examining how employees, managers, and customers interact. Questions addressed should include:

Do they care about one another as people?
Do they respect one another as people?
Do they want to serve one another as people?

If the answer is yes, it shouldn't matter when labels and titles are given. Everyone should be respected because they are human beings and not because they are at a certain level or within a power category. Unfortunately this is not the case. Respect is often given according to how high you are placed on the organizational chart. This impedes the potential for a win/win situation in office life. No matter how many company policies say we should get along and trust one another, they are only words with no life of their own unless the core of the working environment is based on mutual respect, appreciation, and trust. The expression of emotions may vary according to culture, experience, country, and even between individuals. But one thing is certain, anger, fear, unhappiness, hate, love, joy, guilt, and embarrassment are universal. When people are not working as a harmonious unit, there is the potential for miscommunication, unhealthy stereotyping, disloyalty, hidden agendas, and lack of synergy which results in failure for any company.

Dr Daniel Goleman's book, *Emotional Intelligence* discusses how the emotional mind can actually intercept information before it goes to the thinking mind and cause actions or emotional hijackings before the brain has had time for proper interpretation and decision-making. We may have heard terms like: jumping the gun, blowing up, blasting, out of control ... these sayings all point to individuals who lose their tempers and act in ways that are harmful, and after they calm down, regret what they have done. To master this rule is to learn the techniques of self-management which are discussed in this book.

Rule 6:
EQ Development is a Life-Long Endeavour

EQ development requires constant practice, perseverance, hard work, planning, and honesty. Dealing with ourselves is one of the hardest endeavours we can undertake. It is not a quick-fix remedy or a short-term investment. We must dedicate our lives to learning new and better ways to behave and function. Emotional development is not something that can happen overnight. For most of us, it takes years to develop new habits, change old ones and assimilate them into our disposition. Even when we have established EQ there will be ongoing challenges where we are put in contact with people who have not dealt with their emotions. Consequently they will serve as a test to measure our own progress. It is productive to view working with a difficult boss or an unco-operative colleague as an opportunity to practice our EQ skills and provide a role model for others to follow.

Position in life, economic status, or even age do not preclude someone from being a leader. I have seen secretaries, maintenance people, and maids exhibit high EQ competence and their influence was more powerful than those people who held high societal positions, but lacked the inner qualities necessary for personal success. Once you begin on the EQ road it is for life. There is excitement and confidence in knowing that you are working to be a better you. There are road signs along the way which can be useful tips. Watch for them and heed their message when appropriate.

EQ Road Signs

When we are young, we dream of being older because we think this is a time when no one will tell us what to do, we will be free to come and go as we please, and we will have the answers. For many of us who have reached the age we once dreamed of, we now long for the time when we were young and had a more carefree lifestyle. The truth is no age is easy any more, and at each turn along the way we are faced with challenges that are difficult and demanding. We need to remain optimistic because we can survive them and in many cases even triumph. The key is to realize that life is not fair, and to look at it as a journey that has lots of turns, ups and downs, and a few long stretches in all directions. It is not only the final destination we should focus on, we should also embrace the opportunity to grow in wisdom.

The signs along the road of life are clear if we learn to notice them. Remember how we had to learn road signs when first getting our drivers' license? These can be the same signs we use to guide us in our daily lives:

(1) **YIELD.** This is knowing when to slow down and give right of way to someone else. You don't always have to be first and foremost. There are times when it is valuable to let others show us a better way of doing things. The saying, "win the battle but lose the war" can be true when working with people. It feels good to have the last word but when the pendulum swings back to us, it is painful when the other person has the last action. Having inner-control to hold back our impulse toward doing something is a skill worth cultivating. Letting the customer share his unhappiness with a service or product without having to fight back or to defend our position can be productive in obtaining a positive end result. Yielding at times gives you the opportunity to learn and to take time to determine if the avenue you are taking is the right one.

(2)   **STOP (red).** This is knowing when it is important to stop a behaviour, attitude, or way of life which may be detrimental to yourself and others. The spiral effect of anger is a case in point. It starts out with the brain function, then the physical reaction, then the deed. It is important not to fuel anger with negative thoughts, verbal abuse or ranting and raving. Some suggestions to control anger are:

★   *Stop and try to think of a more positive aspect* of a seemingly intolerable situation. This can diffuse our anger and prevent it from spiralling toward rage and outburst. Too often anger accelerates faster than we had wanted, and it is difficult to stop the emotion. In most cases it is better to back off and leave until adequate time has elapsed to cool down.

★   *Visualizing a pleasant thought* can work wonders. A man I worked with had a problem with anger until he used a visualization technique which calmed him down. Whenever he found himself becoming angry he would think of his vacation in Bali. It was one of the most enjoyable times he and his family ever had. The beauty of the water and the tranquillity of the resort where he stayed left a permanent memory in his heart. As soon as he visualized Bali and the water he immediately started calming down to at least a point where he would not cause harm to himself or others.

★   Do not add injury to insult by fanning the flames by going over the scene and adding different and negative perspectives, or by letting others incite you into an emotion that will come back to haunt you. (*See* Secret 7 for more advice.)

(3)   **GO (green).** This is knowing when to take action and when to

leave. A major problem people have is not knowing when to let go. This is true in relationships, arguments, conflicts, unproductive business ventures, and office politics. So often people spend too much time on a problem and not enough on the solution. When we give too much power to other people and live our lives trying to please or measure up to an unreasonable expectation, it leaves us empty and virtually chasing our tails.

Letting go of hurt, anger, guilt, and disappointment is fundamental to having faith, optimism, and belief in yourself. Asking for forgiveness and then forgiving yourself is one of the most important ways to relieve ourselves from the stifling box of complacency and indecision. The pain associated with taking action and not remaining in a comfortable spot is less hurtful in the end than the unhealthy mindsets that creep into our thinking when we are inactive and feeling depressed. To take action means also not letting obstacles in our path be detrimental to our self-esteem. The call to action should be in our spirit.

Jenny, a woman I met in one of my seminars, had a problem letting go of disappointment. When she applied for a job and didn't get it, she spent months trying to get over the feeling of failure. She would feel depressed and after a long while she would go back and try again. It seemed like a pattern was occurring. She would apply for a job, always make it to the final cut and then lose out. After we discussed this in detail we discovered that she was sabotaging herself by assuming that she was not going to get the job. She would always do something to blow her chances. She had refused to let go of the past hurt of not getting what she wanted and it began to build up in her present life. This caused her to be insincere, hesitant, and self-defeating. When she realized what she was doing and the fact that rejection doesn't mean being a failure as a person, she began to take positive action. She changed her paradigm, took action to repair her self-confidence, and after two other attempts she got the job of her dreams.

(4) **CAUTION (yellow).** This is knowing when to watch out for danger or trouble, and when it is advantageous to slow down, assess where you are, and where you are going. In this fast and dynamic world we can be so busy getting ahead that we don't take the time to be cautious of our direction. In business settings observation and analysis of people and situations, and timing when to make decisions are important to surviving and succeeding. Some people jog along not paying attention to the colleague who always seems bored when they are talking, the customer who asks questions about their professional credentials, or the boss who isn't interested in their work. These examples are indications that there is something wrong. Not every jest, comment, or action is cause for worry, but there are times when using your senses as cautionary measures can save you from problems or your inability to deal with them.

(5) **EAST, WEST, NORTH, SOUTH.** These give you an indication of your direction and the opportunity to choose the appropriate course required by providing a correct map. In decision-making the direction is as important as the plan. If we have the right map but receive the wrong direction we will find ourselves lost. This EQ road sign is a symbol for making sure we have direction and an end in mind. Without a destination, we flounder aimlessly leaving ourselves open to toxic and harmful people and their hidden agendas.

(6) **DETOUR.** This is knowing when to take another route and change your direction. One of the worst things we can do to undermine our potential is when we become too set in our ways and rigid in our thoughts. This closes doors of opportunity and stifles fresh ideas. We lock onto comfort and long-standing notions

about life and block information which may give us another way of thinking and feeling. This unwillingness to change direction and take another route has caused destruction in relationships, sabotaged business deals, and generally kept people from growing. This EQ road sign can come in the form of how people label us, for example: inflexible, difficult, and old-fashioned. It can also be seen when businesses and people around us are changing and re-inventing new ways to run their companies while we are still doing business as usual. It is time to examine if we are right to stay on course or should be looking to take a detour.

(7)   **DANGER—drive with caution.** This is knowing when you need to watch where you are going, while watching out for pitfalls along the way that could defeat your efforts. A plan without a strategy for dealing with uncertainties can be like a boat without life-jackets. The sea may be calm one minute, but when it is rough how will we cope? Driving with caution is being smart and anticipating the dangers along the way. This will ensure you do not take things for granted.

A friend of mine was so excited about the thought of having an investor for her newly-established company that she didn't take the time to investigate his background or to draw up a proper agreement. Caught up in the moment she signed the agreement in haste. When the company began making money the problems started. There were disagreements over the administration and personnel matters, mission, and financial spending. This escalated into anger, mistrust, and heated arguments. Finally, they went to court where she lost. She hadn't protected herself from the beginning by preparing for problems that could arise. The honeymoon of the joint venture was wonderful but the divorce was horrible and very costly to her in the end.

(8)   **ROAD BLOCKS.** These are knowing the problem areas that can slow down your success, or even preventing it from happening. Some road blocks are unavoidable and some you can't get over. The critical factor is to know they are there, and to compensate for the outcomes. There are very few ventures that don't have some sort of stumbling blocks to overcome. Road blocks can serve as important signs that a bigger issue is brewing or that a short-term matter can be dealt with fairly quickly. Interaction problems between people usually fall into the category of stumbling blocks until they go unattended and become major conflicts. Raising our antennas and being mindful of all barriers toward success can be a useful tool in heading them off before they actually grow into prominent concerns.

(9)   **MPH.** This is knowing when to go faster and when to go slower. Your speed can determine the quality as well as the quantity of your progress. The rhythm of life calls for knowing the speed upon which to pursue activities. In business situations the waiting game for deals to close can becomes tedious and full of anxiety, as we ask ourselves such questions as, "how long should I wait before I act?" or "how fast should I progress?" In personal relationships we ask the same questions, should I let her know how much I care or is it too soon?" and "when is the right time to let him kiss me or will he think I am too anxious?" All of these questions demand the same kind of introspection that the other EQ road signs require— watching and listening for clues that tell us at what speed to proceed.

I was in a business meeting with a new client whom I had never talked with before. I had given a presentation and was now waiting to learn of his reaction. The meeting pace was so slow yet I knew that it was important to work at the tempo of the meeting. The client was a Singaporean businessman who wanted to learn more about me before discussing my presentation. We spent a lot of time in small talk. It appeared to be small but was very big because he was assessing my sincerity, knowledge, and honesty—all important virtues in a business arrangement. I took my time and got to know him. When he was satisfied of who I was and what I really wanted with his company, we went on to discuss the presentation. I got the job. If my miles per hour rate was not in sync with his and if I had increased speed instead of going at a slower pace, I would have lost a good client. Learning how to adjust to the tempo of our interactions is a skill worth cultivating.

(10) **REST STOPS.** This is knowing when to take time out to replenish your mind and body, and when to give yourself space to regroup before starting over. Learning to use the EQ road signs toward personal and professional growth will help you to make better decisions. Signs along your journey of life are there if you take the time to observe them and follow their advice. Effective self-management not only allows us to govern our emotional and intellectual abilities in a more productive manner, it also endows us with the wisdom and patience to understand the external factors that have great importance to our achieving success. Time out to smell the roses, take in the beauty of nature, spend quality time with our children, and really talk with our spouses can make a big difference in how we charge up for battle, and do not succumb to the temptation to give in to pressure, turmoil, and workplace demands. In reality, professional life does not have to be a battle at all. It can be a growing and empowering experience for all of us. Work can be the means which help us take the time to rest, to receive the personal help we need, and to enjoy the fruits of our labour. A strong body, a healthy and peaceful mindset will do wonders when dealing with the dynamics in the world of work.

WHAT IS A TOXIC PERSON?

The word "toxic" is defined in the dictionary as "pertaining to, affected with, or caused by a toxin or poison." Translating this to people means individuals who through their actions, deeds, behaviours, and attitudes bring a form of venom that seeps into an environment and obstructs the positive and productive elements. These people can have a pleasant veneer but underneath carry a motive that is self-centred, negative, and obtrusive. Other toxic people visually and verbally let it be known who they are and what they intend to do. They incite fear, anger, and frustration in those they meet. Discussions with them turn into arguments and their strength is derived from an ability to cause dissension among and between people. They usually leave a trail of hurt, pain and antagonistic relationships. You see them in meetings undermining the group or in positions of power where people have to dodge their arrows and fend off contempt. They blow up, get even, fight, and manipulate to the point where the office becomes a battleground and a place where General Patton's warfare tactics are needed just to get through the day. In many cases, toxic people do not realize they give off an unpleasant toxin and would be the first to say, "I did not mean to do this." How do you deal with them and win? The following examples will illustrate how to do so.

1. THE FOUR BEST WAYS TO DEAL WITH TOXIC PEOPLE

EXAMPLE 1:
THE SUPERVISOR

I had a supervisor who gained sheer delight by making his staff's professional life miserable. I survived this job and actually learned a great deal from this person when I accepted the truism that *we are here for a reason and each experience is there to teach us something.* The key is to find out what it is we are supposed to learn and pray for wisdom. For me, it was to strengthen my ability to face conflict, to sharpen my skills and better my communication abilities. I also learned a lot about myself and the challenges of working with people. We often want the gold ring or the reward but we are under the assumption that it can be done without our personal development. It's not enough to have the academic qualifications, we need the human credentials that are only obtained in the societal classrooms.

By turning an uncomfortable situation into a positive one, we can prepare ourselves to deal with the many challenges along the way. Toxic people rely on our ego getting in the way of our logic. My former supervisor would put his staff down by asking questions which were rhetorical, such as, "are you stupid, why would you do something so ineffective?", or "why did I hire you?" What he wanted was a sign that you were buying into his assertion of being a failure as opposed to having failed to meet a goal. He wanted people to be intimidated enough to fail in the long run. This gave him power and excitement and allowed him to control adults. The reality of the situation was that he usually gave incomplete instructions and the results produced by the staff which did not match what he actually wanted. The lesson here is to be prepared, know all issues, delve deeper for answers, better phrase the questions and think in a commonsense manner. The toxic supervisor was bright and knew the answers before he asked the questions. He just wasn't going to teach what he knew. His game was to make a person clarify the questions, then find the answers and defend their professional decisions. He respected astuteness, organized analysis presented in a direct and confident manner. For that reason the time spent under his employ, although stressful, was useful and provided a productive learning environment. Toxic people tend to deal in rhetoric, insinuation, and insecurity. They hide behind an air of superiority which is intended to place you on the defensive instead of the offensive.

During my tenure working for this supervisor I taught myself to tap into my inner resources of self-esteem and self-management, which have been the catalyst for recognizing my own power and leading the way for me to help empower others. The supervisor's actions were mean-spirited and unprofessional. I am not suggesting that people become this way to provide inspiration and experiences for others. However, it is critical to remember in situations like this one that the problem belonged to the supervisor, and there was a need to become skilled in dealing with an individual of this nature. It was important that I did not allow myself to take on his weaknesses by acting as he acted. Rather, I found ways to learn and draw upon my strengths which in turn made my own talents clearer.

When dealing with negative people you must remain calm, direct, and professional. In confrontational situations, state facts and remain on the issue at hand. Toxic people gain their strength by trying to make you angry and unbalanced so that your thinking becomes emotionally charged and irrational. They recoil from self-composure and self-confidence.

Example 2:
The Story of Mr Young

A friend of mine, Mr Young, exhibited an excellent example of how to diffuse a situation. A toxic person's goal was to turn a discussion into a nasty argument and make him feel at fault, when in fact it was the other way around. Mr Young was summoned to his colleagues' office to talk about a letter that he had sent which his colleague did not like. It outlined how after several telephone calls and E-mails the colleague had refused to return his messages and neglected to provide Mr Young with vital information, causing a delay in providing service to his clients. Upon entering his colleagues' office, Mr Young noticed that the man would not look up from his desk and continued to write even after my friend had greeted him. It was obvious to Mr Young that this was a power strategy. He remained standing and stared at his colleague who became uncomfortable by the silence and immediately looked up. He began to point his finger and accuse Mr Young of not respecting him by putting in writing the fact that he had not acknowledged his request and it was harmful to clients. Mr Young remained calm and professional and addressed him in a forthright way as he reviewed the course of events which led up to the letter. Even after several interruptions by the colleague who made personal attacks against his character, Mr Young still continued to state the facts. Finally when the accusations became too belligerent Mr Young countered in a forceful voice, "no matter what cheap shots you aim at me it will not make me angry or change the course of events. Your comments and mannerisms are unprofessionalism and rude. You have not shown by concrete evidence anything to support your claim, you have chosen instead to use personal attacks to deal with me." Mr Young continued, "Before this is all over you will either respect me or learn from me." The colleague became unbalanced when the facts governed the discussion and with no counter points his argument was exposed as petty and insincere. Realizing his power tactics and nasty comments had not worked and his contention was shallow, he retreated and tried to defend himself by saying that he had wanted to help but was pre-empted by the letter. This was an attempt to shift the blame away from himself. Mr Young, noticing the attempt, did not wish revenge as he received gratification in the retreat itself and decided to work on a resolution.

The resolution was how to get the needed resources to his clients. If Mr Young had joined in on the pettiness and unprofessional behaviour of his colleague, or allowed his ego or emotions to drive the situation there would be no resolution. Further bickering could have led to physical altercations or supervisory input could have resulted. Several weeks later, Mr Young needed additional supplies from this colleague and after one written request, he received his answer and his work proceeded on schedule.

In office environments, everyone reacts differently when faced with difficult and confrontational situations. For some, the lesson would be to find another job and fast, but for most of us this is not a productive alternative. I believe strongly in the strength and resourcefulness of our minds. We can look at our cup as half empty or half full. We can choose to believe that grapes, although sour at first, can become the loveliest of fine wines with time and perseverance. The secret to inner power is the realization that we can make decisions as to what we think, how we feel, how we respond, and whether we use the dynamic duo of our Mind and Emotion (M.E.)

Using M.E. to deal with people requires taking responsibility for our actions and combining emotional strength with mind-power to remain focused on a higher mission in life. The ultimate goal of M.E. is to move forward in an optimistic attitude rather than venture off in the direction of petty details or attitudes that diminish human relationships. It is positive to want to be the best "you", and to make improvements where necessary. However, when your self-recriminations prevent you from growing or moving forward then they become a personal liability. We must work toward understanding ourselves as much as understanding the needs of others. It can be detrimental to seek perfection as it is also unproductive in trying to place blame. We have the capacity to be the best that God created and we owe it to ourselves to put our energies in that direction.

Example 3:
The Psychology Game

Ron was a man of action who wanted to control and keep everyone always guessing what he was thinking and feeling. Just when you thought you knew him he turned chameleon and changed personality. He kept people off guard with this skill. His colleagues found themselves changing to fit his moods. They were intimidated, and as one woman put it, it was as if she were a schoolgirl trying to please her teacher. Ron's behaviour worked for him for many years and he rose up the ladder because of his skill and the fact that people feared and revered his abilities. He had created an image of a fearless warrior. This made his enemies respect him and subordinates cow down to him. One day he met his match. Peter, a man from a competitive advertising firm was bidding for the same client as Ron. They learned of each other and began to wage a psychological game of power plays. Ron changed colours more often than usual trying to offset his competitor, while Peter used manipulation tactics that rivalled any Hollywood B-rated movie. People around them, caught up in the energy of these two competing powers, were stunned by their intensity and were busy weathering the storm they had created.

What Peter and Ron had not realized was that their psychological warfare had reached the client. Their unprofessional antics brought a showdown in the office of the client they were courting. What happened was a total transformation. They became friendly and professional toward one another and covered up their competitiveness which had bordered on a lack of ethics. The client became confused. What finally took place was that Peter, unbeknownst to Ron, had lined up 12 people who hated him and had them write confidential letters to the client after the meeting explaining how he changed his exterior to fit an occasion. Peter had the same enemies but Ron had underestimated the limits Peter would go to win the client. Ron lost the account and never knew why.

Four lessons from this story for toxic people:

- You gather more enemies than supporters. When given the chance, people will turn against you.

- Never overestimate your power. Just as you went up the ladder so you can come right down. Even the more devious plans can have a flaw. Ron's flaw was that he thought he was the champion of spite but it turned out to be Peter.

- Don't assume that because people appear defenceless, they may not retaliate. Someday they may strike back. When people have been pushed to the limit they usually rebel. This rebellion will either come in the form of outbursts, resignation of positions, telling the world of a person's deviousness, or standing up to them with an army in support.

- In the end evil deeds do more harm to the doer than to the recipient. The price a toxic person pays is possible havoc on their health, personal life, and eventually career. Unless they are totally without conscious, guilt, or fear, this constant act of making other people's lives miserable will boomerang back into their lives which will begin to unravel by their own doing.

Example 4:
The Seeds Pamela Sowed

Pamela had beauty and charm and used each to the fullest. She spent more time figuring out how to undermine her co-worker, Denise, than working on her own success. She was jealous of Denise's popularity with the staff and the fact that Denise was secretly engaged to their boss, Paul. They kept it a secret to avoid making others feel uncomfortable around Denise in the office. They planned to marry the next year and Denise was going to stop working and make a home for them. Pamela had always wanted a successful man and hated everything she thought Denise was able to get. After all, she felt it should have been hers because she was prettier and had more personality. One day Pamela decided to make a pass at Paul at a conference they were both attending. Paul fell into her trap and spent the night with her. The next day he was full of remorse, ashamed of his mistake. Pamela saw this as her big chance. She demanded that he leave Denise for her. To her surprise, he said no and expressed his love for Denise. Pamela promised not to tell Denise and pretended that the brief affair had meant nothing to her. But her toxic deceitful nature grew. She began to make subtle hints around Denise who already suspected from Paul's attitude that something was wrong. Pamela played on this sudden insecurity and hinted at the possibility of another woman. This caused pain to Denise and resulted in friction between herself and Paul. Pamela spread a rumour about herself and Paul around the office and soon everyone was talking about it.

Unaware that Denise and Paul were engaged, some staff members told Denise of the affair between Pamela and Paul. Unable to deal with Pamela's deceit and Paul's betrayal, Denise went running out of the office. Paul and Denise broke up, and after a long time Pamela and Paul got married.

Sadly, Paul's inability to accept his mistake and the guilt that resulted caused him to drink. This led to abusive behaviour on his part as he expressed his resentment against Pamela for taking him away from the woman he truly loved.

To Pamela's horror, Paul turned into an alcoholic who beat her and treated her with contempt. She had two children with him and lived a lonely and unhappy life. People that knew Pamela were taken aback at how she had changed. The once beautiful woman was now old, hard, and unhappy. Without a career and money she found herself staying for the money. In the end Pamela reaped what she had sown.

Toxic ways can backfire on the person and actually cause them the most pain. As in the case of Pamela, she had caused suffering to others and her life turned into one of misery. In an office setting, people who bring about unhappiness and anxiety in others are using their emotional cleverness for the wrong reason. Gifts of persuasion should be used for good. Too often we are unaware of a person's true nature and will fall into the trap of believing in them.

Con artists, false prophets, and conniving leaders can induce people to do things that are unnatural, unhealthy, and potentially dangerous. It is important in EQ success to develop the skill of recognizing people who are not honest and whose mission it is to rob you of your dignity and self-esteem.

The best way to deal with toxic people are the following:

(1) **Do not let toxic people rob you of your personal power.** No matter who they are, or what position they hold, they have no right to attack you as a person. When they do, you don't have to believe them. They are counting on you to diminish your own self-esteem and lower your confidence. Toxic people can't stand individuals who believe in themselves and are not be shaken by their games.

(2) **Maintain control when faced with a toxic person.** They use intimidating methods to control a person. By not giving in to fear, anger, tears, or shame lowers their effectiveness. They win when you lose your emotional balance and inner harmony. They actually fear people who stand tall and do not falter when they roar their meanness.

(3) **Do not pay too much attention to toxic people**. Listen and evaluate the information carefully, but do not let what they say influence you. Be discriminate in how much you use. Denise allowed Pamela to tap into her insecurities and gave her too much importance. A better way would have been to talk with Paul and build a better communication with him and not let Pamela's influence push her away from the man she loved.

(4) **Stand up for yourself when dealing with toxic people**. What they count on most is that their shrewdness and power will diminish you and force you into submission. Express your viewpoints professionally and with passion so that they know that you mean what you say and will not back down.

(5) **Build support among your colleagues**. Be a star player and build alliances which will support you when faced with a toxic person. These alliances can be helpful in getting rid of toxic people. The worst position to be in is the lone ranger fighting alone. Seek advice from select others.

(6) **Watch your back**. Make sure you are observant and informed about what is going on in the office setting. Do not leave anything to chance. Maintain a constant flow of information so that you can become proactive instead of reacting to what is happening to you. Through your alliances you can stay ahead of the game.

(7) **Know your enemy**. Keep abreast of what the toxic person is doing. Do not become complacent. It is easy to fall victim to them when confrontation occurs. Never fall into the trap of sharing information or secrets with a toxic person. It will come back to hurt you. Avoid sharing anything special and make sure anything you put in writing is suitable for public consumption. A rule of

thumb is never say anything about someone you wouldn't say to them personally. This will limit the toxic person from ruining your relationships and reputation.

(8) **When your boss is the toxic person.** The key word is professionalism. Do your job well, do your homework and stand your ground. Understand the organizational structure and the unwritten rules within the environment. Find mentors to help you and keep a paper trail. Be an EQ star by making positive relationships with colleague and customers. Make yourself indispensable by being the kind of employee you would want if the company belonged to you.

(9) **Do not enter into the toxic game**. One thing that a toxic person can do best is to be toxic. Unless you are as toxic it is best not to become involved in their schemes. It is more effective to maintain your principles and code of conduct. This strength unsettles them and is useful in reducing their impact.

(10) **Dealing with toxic customers**. A toxic customer is different. You have to understand where they are coming from, what they expect and determine the type of aggression they are projecting. Being as rude or defensive as they are will surely put you in a losing position. Crying and becoming so fearful that you can't function will also not help. Maintaining your composure, empathizing with their concern, and respecting them as customers are the best ways. Second, it is helpful to know your job well and are able to call on resources fast so they know you can back any claims up. Above all learn how to manage your own emotions, so that you apply the most productive response to the situation. A conflict is only created when you enter into it. Don't forget that you are dealing with a disgruntled, perhaps rude but valuable customer.

Screening/Selection Process: Choosing What You Internalize

Since the technological boom we have been bombarded with enormous amounts of information stemming from a variety of sources. Imagine looking at a busy street in New York City during rush hour with all the visual stimuli and noise levels. Think of this scene going on in fast motion. If we internalize everything that we hear and see, we could become nervous wrecks for trying to deal with it all. Screening the information we receive and selecting from it what we internalize is a mind-saving management technique. Once you have done this, your mind will test your sincerity by resurfacing the original concern. It is at this point that you must say again, "this is not worth my frustration." Not all things are important enough for us to worry about, vent over for long periods of time, or affect us in the first place. Screening what we are exposed to, deciding what we will keep internally, and throwing out what is unnecessary takes combining discipline, logic and impulse control. The more we learn to do it, the easier it becomes.

1. Unproductive Habits

Unnecessary worry is a habit that we picked up along the way and can be broken if we follow these steps:

(1)   **When you have decided that something is out of your control** or is not worth your time you should tell yourself "this is not something I am going to worry about," say STOP to this self-defeating thought.

(2) **When there is a problem that is of concern,** allow yourself to think about it, analyse it, place the appropriate emotion to it, try to resolve it and then get rid of it. There is nothing more fruitless then letting an old wound that has been treated, reappear as if it has just been hurt. Letting go is one of the most difficult things for human beings to do. We savour the bad sometimes longer then the good and we refuse to move on. When we give ourselves a specific time frame to grieve, release anger or hurt, we must take charge of our minds and direct it to release the bothersome thought and fill it with productive and current realities. This takes combining knowledge (what we know to be true), discipline (maintaining the reality), desire (wanting to do it), and skill (know how to make it happen) to form a positive habit.

(3) **Look at any event or situation as an opportunity to grow** and try not to make the same mistakes again. Treating problems as learning curves will enable you to forgive yourself when you are at fault, and also to take responsibility for learning from the mistake. If we do not use a system for dealing with the stimuli we receive it can leave us disoriented, confused, and out of control. Having goals and a direction for your life will ensure that as you receive the tremendous amount of knowledge each day you will be better able to sort through it quickly, select what is productive, and keep or dispose of it.

Example

Andre was a person who internalized everything. If the gas attendant was not friendly one day he would spend an hour wondering what his problem was. He would dwell on news accounts of others tragedy to the point where he would dream about it at night. His friends' problems became his and he spent most of his free time thinking and rethinking about everything that he said and did throughout the week. Nothing escaped his view. He took on causes that were vital but not relevant to him and he paid attention to all details no matter how small.

Andre's self-talk and thought processes were working overtime and it was no wonder he talked in his sleep. He rarely relaxed because everything was in his domain to analyse and evaluate. He wasn't particularly nervous, but he was self-absorbed in a way that prevented him from enjoying spontaneity and peace of mind. As a result he went from one crisis to another. One day he was wondering what had happened to the woman who just walked into a pizza shop to pick up her dinner and had broken her leg. At this point his sister stopped him and looked him square in the eye and said, "Andre, you spend so much time worrying and fussing over others that you spend no time getting to know yourself or developing your own potential." She further commented that he did not have to take on all of the world's problems. It was all right to let something go unnoticed and his evaluation was not always necessary.

He was very shaken by her response. He told her that he never realized he could be selective about the things he internalized and that he need not worry so much about the behaviours of others. He never imagined that he had a choice. Andre told his sister that her words had actually provided a release from his obsessive habit. His sister's strength and constructive feedback was a catalyst for helping him understand how to manage his intake of information. As the weeks passed, Andre began to give himself permission to be freer and not to overload his mind with every aspect of life. He now believes that he doesn't have to give emotion or weight to everything around him. He now laughs more, sees the humour in life, and is less obsessive. It is necessary for us to sometimes give ourselves a break and the opportunity to lighten up.

CREATING PERSONAL EQ EVEN IN A LOW EQ Office ENVIRONMENT

How many of us are excited and look forward to going into the office? Those of us who are have found an interest, or meaning to our work. The office is a place where we can accomplish and feel satisfaction. It may be the challenge and intensity of accomplishing a goal that makes the office a dynamic place to come each day. But for many people the workplace is not a pleasant environment. On Sunday evening stress starts to creep in because the next day is work. As I talk with many employees and managers, they tell me their work would be fun and challenging if it weren't for the office environment. In such atmospheres there is negative competition, backbiting, hidden agendas, and insincerity. How can anyone find happiness in places like these? You can. But it starts with your personal EQ.

(1) **Personal Paradigm.** This is your internal and external viewpoint. How you see yourself in relation to others makes a difference in how you interact with people in your office. If you do not hold yourself in high esteem, what people say and do will affect you to the point where you are diminished professionally. If your self-image is poor then you won't believe that you are likeable and that people find you have a nice personality. With this attitude, you tend to be shy, and afraid to speak up in meetings. This results in people not fully knowing your potential.

(2) **Personal Conditioning.** This includes your expectation, vision, and environment. As we gain experience, we form our vision, expectation, and preferences for working and how to be treated. If we have the expectation that we should be a manager and we are a secretary, our vision will not match our situation and therefore

our work situation will not fulfil us. Some people enjoy working in more supervised and smaller units and when placed in larger and more flexible environments they feel uncomfortable and unable to cope well. Knowing what you want out of life, how you see yourself, and what is the best environment for you are important considerations when looking for a career. Many of us change over time and what we thought we wanted is no longer an ideal so we find ourselves in places that no longer fulfil our needs. When this occurs we have to exert personal leadership in finding a better and more suitable position.

(3)   **Self-leadership.** This includes our locus of control, mission, norms, and behaviours. If we believe we have efficacy and the ability to manage our own destiny to some extent then we are more likely to find happiness in positions that may not be ideal for us at a given time. The thought of not having control, or the capacity to make changes is often more upsetting than the circumstances we find ourselves in. Exerting personal power can be stimulating and comforting to many. The next area in self-leadership is having a mission. If we don't know where we are going we can't complain when we don't get there. To define who we are and what we want out of life is a prerequisite for determining our purpose. The norms/ behaviours are the standards that we have established for how we are going to behave, treat ourselves and others, and generally conduct our lives. Self-leadership is empowerment in the fullest of terms and can only be activated when we take control of ourselves.

(4)   **Self-management.** This involves our character, the giants that loom in us, and our wellness. Our character houses our principles and values. If our character is weak, we will fall into the trap of doing what goes against our principles and will become involved in deeds that will eventually take a toll on our inner well-being.

The giants are those toxic and hidden problems that loom tall in our minds and dictate our actions all too many times. The longer we allow a giant to go unaddressed, the bigger, more imposing, and aggressive it will become. Problems do not go away only the friends and colleagues who can't tolerate what we bring into the workplace. Wellness is taking care of ourselves. Deal with your giants, spend time resting and replenishing your spiritual life. Prayer, meditation, exercising, and staying healthy are important ingredients in being able to manage your emotions and work life.

PART THREE
EQ SELF-MANAGEMENT

Internal Organization: a Matter of Perspective

An event is simply that until you make your response, then it becomes an outcome.

How many of us spend our lives trying to hide the fact that we do not feel equipped to handle the pressure and people who cause us stress? It is not a good feeling to believe that you are unable to manage yourself or others in situations that get out of hand. Too often we could have avoided problems if we had only thought instead of acted. How many times have you said, "my emotions got the better of me," or "I don't know what came over me" or "I should have seen that coming."

Many of us sit on the sideline afraid to take the necessary risks that would improve our lives because we are not sure how to tackle the outcome of our decisions. I remember as a child my parents labelled me emotional and in many ways I was. Their favourite saying was that I carried my heart on my sleeve. Life is sometimes like a poker game. If you are not taught how to play your hand, or how to manage your attitude so that the other player doesn't know your game, you will invariably give away your hand. Or even worse, you will lose the game of building relationships needed to accomplish your goals.

Managing our emotions doesn't mean we should be deceitful or manipulative. It means that we know ourselves and how to effectively deal with people and circumstances. To have empathy for others is a valuable asset in most careers and building a win/win situation is a key in negotiation but remains one of the most difficult goals to achieve. As part of an international society we are conditioned to compete and to win which means someone has to lose. To lose or to fail is not positive and doesn't feel good. However, failing and losing at times can be one of the best ways to learn and prosper if it doesn't become a habit. Most experienced people will advise you based on the mistakes they have made. The best lessons in life are those which have taught us how to deal with pain and suffering. This may sound dramatic, but placed in various contexts, it is at the heart of our emotional instability. Pain and suffering may result from losing a loved one, not getting the job of our dreams, working with dangerous and toxic people, not being able to manage the stress and fear. The best instruction during our journey in life often comes from those people who have hurt or cheated us. The fork in the road which determines our success or failure depends on how we manage emotions, read a situation, and how we manage the emotions in others.

We can break away from sabotaging our relationships by placing intelligence on a par with our internal make-up. Cultivating emotional intelligence should be an ongoing activity which will prepare us for developing competencies to handle ourselves in good times, as well as bad. The ability to master harmonizing our rational (thinking) with our often irrational (emotional) side is a worthy goal.

It is always easier to concentrate on the superficial development of our outer image. Working on our character and emotions are most difficult. We can be our own worst enemy. During your journey of personal development, some people may argue that emotions are not irrational. In some cases this is true. Showing love, exhibiting grief when losing a loved one, or giving of ourselves for a worthy cause even when it may delay our own individual recognition are not irrational acts in a caring sense. It appears irrational to people who fail to understand or allow themselves to feel empathy, love or compassion. The world is filled with people who stop feeling for whatever reason. There are also many of us who can't identify what we are feeling as we experience it. When left unattended emotions can build into stronger and less controllable impulses to act.

Example

A woman was fired on the spot by a brutal and unfair boss. She left the office upset at what had happened to her. She wondered how she was going to tell her husband and family and started to fret about her reputation once everyone found out she had been fired. As her self-talk continued to probe these questions, her emotions built up. Her nervous system in high gear, her *amydala* (emotional centre) started looking for ways to unleash the pile-up of adrenaline. Getting on the subway, she sat next to a woman with a baby. The baby began to cry and cry. The woman, feeling that she wanted to scream found her blood pressure mounting. The palms of her hands were balmy and her anger was aroused. Finally, she couldn't stand to hear another scream and suddenly jumped up out of her seat and bumped into a man standing in front of her. She started yelling obscenities at him. He yelled back, and she started hitting him with her handbag. The train stopped and passengers, trying to get off, were detained by the fight that had now started between the man and the woman. Some passengers tried to stop them but it was not possible. Finally the man got off the train and the woman started crying louder than the baby. At the next stop she got off and ran away into the streets.

Some of us may say this woman "lost it". In a sense she did. Her emotional centre became so overloaded brought on by the baby's cry, that it bypassed her neocortex, which houses her thinking and logic functions, and went straight to her amydala by way of her thalamus and her prefrontal lobes which triggered a distress signal to her brain which resulted in her outburst. She was totally unaware of what was happening to her and became overwhelmed and could not channel her emotions effectively. In fact, as she told the story she called herself a "woman possessed" because of her lack of self-control. As she let off steam it actually escalated. As demonstrated it is not good to vent.

Venting can actually give strength to the growing funnel of anger or despair. What would have saved the woman from the emotional distress that day would have been if she had learned to manage her emotions. This means to be able to identify what is really troubling you and the source of concern. We tend to dwell on the emotion itself which may not be the true feeling. At first the woman who lost her job believed she was feeling upset and frustrated because she had failed and that she worried what her family and friends would say. However, as she later analysed her behaviour she realized that underneath it all, she was furious at the indignation of what had happened to her and how her boss had harassed her for so long about her job. The woman could have avoided the inappropriate fight on the train if she had realized that she was feeling angry and hurt. It would have been appropriate for her to take time to step back from the situation until she was more in control of her emotions. After such a pause, her self-talk could have helped her understand that leaving a toxic working environment was much better than staying and that she would survive. If she had just taken the time to process the entire situation she could grow from the experience.

Ask yourself this question: would you want to work for a person who is capable, people-oriented, confident and highly motivated to succeed, or would you prefer a brilliant but guarded, inhibited, and unavailable person who only relates to you in terms of information? For most of us, we would chose an open person with people-oriented qualities. When emotion is not channelled properly and goes unattended, it can result in a response or action which when rationally examined will bring negative or devastating effects.

Combining our thinking mind with our emotional mind is most important in relationships and in work environments. Functioning in a reactive state limits one's ability to make the right choices. Failure to understand our emotional make-up can erode our personal effectiveness to the point where we feel depressed and unmotivated to rise to our potential.

Four Ways to Improve Our Emotional State

1. Self-Talk

Our "self-talk" governs how we perceive the world around us. It affects our attitudes and determines our emotional state. It's that inner voice that dictates our response to situations, our interactions with people, and our reaction to adversity or challenges we face. When we play tennis or any sport, our self-talk can either help us or hurt us. If we believe we will miss the ball and not hit it over the net, chances are we won't. If we believe we can hit the ball, learn technical skills, and practice with determination, we more than likely will. Our inner voice works overtime telling us what to do and what to think. With the proper training we can learn to make our thoughts our best ally. Without effective maintenance our inner voice can turn our outlook to a negative one which is unproductive and self-destructive.

2. Family Background and Life Experiences

Our family background and experiences in life have given us a mind filled with a wealth of assimilated viewpoints, biases, and thought-conditioning which we draw upon at any given moment to determine our interpretations of events and actions.

Often it is not what was done to us by others that determines our response but how we evaluate an individual action in relation to our self-worth or our value as a person. For example, if someone remarks that our suggestion was stupid, the disturbance occurs when we begin to think about how the other person views our intelligence. Our ego gets bruised. Questions arise such as, "Is this person disrespectful of me?" or "will others think I am stupid?" We draw upon our experiences and what we believe is the correct way to be treated to interpret a person's remarks.

We often put more importance on another person's perspective of us than we do on our understanding of ourselves. This is not to say we shouldn't take constructive criticism from those who are being helpful. We should be careful not to allow the words of some who have negative motives to control our reactions and undermine our behaviours. If a woman who has little credibility makes a negative comment about our hair or our intelligence, it should not offset us to the point where we look down on ourselves. Instead, first, as the old saying goes, "look at the source" and then ask yourself, "am I giving this person too much power over how I think and feel?" Finally, "do I allow anyone to control me?"

3. Developing Inner Strength

This will enable us to fend off the judgements of people who may be jealous, rude, self-centred, prejudiced, fearful, or have low self-esteem themselves. We will build the strength needed to direct our own actions and move toward reaching our potential. We will learn to see how insignificant negative comments or feelings of others do not add real value to us as people. Negative people have influence over us only when we give up our own inner power. It takes a conscious effort to deal with negative or "hateful" people. These individuals usually try to diminish our light, draw out our insecurities, and break our positive spirit. Some are very obvious in their devious behaviour while others are more clever. One strong and effective defence against people who try and break our spirit is to believe in our own value, understand what we need to work on personally and professionally, and never let their input get in the way of our progress. We should celebrate in our own uniqueness and the capabilities to create a positive and fulfilling inner light, to envision all of our possibilities, the strength to overcome adversity and the ability, to turn dreams into realities.

4. AN EXERCISE

As you read this illustration, put yourself in this man's position. Imagine walking into a restaurant and seeing your best friend having lunch with your wife who had declined lunch with you stating she had a PTA meeting at school. All of a sudden you find yourself out of control. You rush over to their table, yelling obscenities and accusing them of having an affair to the horror of the people sitting at the nearby tables. You proceed to hit your best friend and poignantly state to your wife that she had better get a good lawyer.

What's wrong with this picture? Take a moment before you write down your answers.

1. What was wrong with the way the husband handled the situation?

   _____

   _____

   _____

   _____

   _____

2. What triggered this response?

   _____

   _____

_____

_____

_____

3.   What would you have done? Would you have dealt with the situation better? If not, how could you improve your behaviour?

_____

_____

_____

_____

_____

The following is a discussion of what took place. See if you have similar thoughts and determine what can be learned from this illustration.

Discussion

There are many scenarios that can be attributed to this illustration. The question is which response would have been most productive and how could the husband have found out the truth in a more effective way. To begin with it appears that the wife did not tell her husband the truth. She should have been at school or should she? Perhaps the meeting was called off and she decided to treat herself to lunch. While eating alone, she ran into her husband's best friend and asked him to join her. Or, as she was leaving the house, she received an urgent telephone call from the best friend asking her to meet him to discuss a personal problem.

Since he was just a friend why would it matter to her husband, right? Perhaps she tried to call her husband to ask him to join them, but he was not in the office. Or, they are lovers secretly meeting. These or many other reasons could account for why his wife and best friend were together.

In your answer did you consider any of these reasons or others as to why they were together? Did you decide to gather more information before making an assumption, or did you do as the man in the illustration had done: immediately believed that they were up to no good?

Let's explore further what happened.

- The husband neglected to consider any option other than betrayal.

- He let his emotions and one detail that was inconsistent cloud his thinking and he jumped to a conclusion.

- He didn't wait to find out the truth, he didn't consider the fact that they had both been loyal to him over the years, and he didn't ask them what was happening. He simply went from detail to emotion to conclusion to action. What he left out of this important formula was:

> Information + Explanation + Verification.

- It turned out that his wife and his best friend had planned a surprise 45th birthday party for him that weekend and met to finalize the program. To his later dismay, even after apologizing to both parties, the outcome brought tension between he and his wife because she now felt he didn't trust her and his friend because he never gave them a chance to explain.

- The lack of trust and respect and not giving them the benefit of the doubt, were the driving forces in almost ruining the husband's relationships. All of this happened because he hadn't learned to manage himself. Through his internal disorganization came the outburst which caused havoc.

- Had he calmed down and thought about the prior week, he might have noticed unusual activities. For example, the florist shop manager dropped by with an arrangement sample for his wife. All of their champagne glasses were sitting on the dining-room table, the gardener came earlier than usual and was planting additional flowers. Although his wife had explanations for the activities, he still thought there was much more movement than usual in the house, but dismissed it. Had he stopped and given himself time to manage all of the stimuli that was coming into his mind, and think logically, he may have put the pieces together with the fact that his birthday was on the next Saturday.

Daniel Goleman terms this emotional reaction as an "emotional hijacking". We have an emotional explosion when the limbic brain signals an emergency and bypasses the neocortex–our thinking, rational brain. This short-circuit approach is brought about when we perceive yourself to be in an emotionally charged situation and your eye, ear, or any sensory system signals the thalamus, and from there your amygdala (emotional centre). Most of the time our senses will send signals to the thalamus and from there sensory processing areas of the neocortex will sort out information to give meaning to the subject and from there we make a decision. This is usually done with more reason. The short-cut acts without the time to examine what is happening in more detail. In some cases a quick emotional reaction can save your life. For example, if you are walking by yourself and notice someone following you and you immediately run to an area where there are people this quick action may save you from danger. Through evolution our brains have been conditioned to deal with danger and uncertainty rapidly. These tools have served mankind for the last 50,000 years. These "emotional hijackings" do not serve us well today and will not in the generations to come. Like the husband in the above illustration, if we do not manage our emotions and develop an awareness of our biological propensities for acting, we can live a lifetime feeling badly about our actions, and wondering why we did not get ahead even though we were intellectually smart, or why our relationships were always in turmoil.

An important element to self-management is to understand our character weaknesses as well as our strengths. If you have a tendency toward having a low self-esteem, you must remember old self-depreciating attitude will influence your behaviour. The husband in this illustration would need to examine his personal qualities and his self-esteem to determine if he needs to build a strong inner foundation which would enable him to be free to establish open and positive relationships. He would also need to evaluate whether his own actions and attitudes make him mistrustful of others. In order to enhance our self-management skills it is important to understand the fundamental components and how to make it better work for us. There are four processes of creating a more balanced and effective way of managing ourselves which can be valuable as we deal with everyday situations.

SELF-MANAGEMENT COMPONENTS

Self management is the process of:

(1) **Sorting through our many thoughts and feelings** to provide us with an understanding of our internal make-up, and the hot spots that trigger our jealousy, anger, fear, bias, insecurity, and

discomfort. Self-management gives us the basis for working on new ways to think and act so that we will be more effective and proactive rather then reactive when dealing with people and circumstances. So often when something happens to us we are so overcome that we respond immediately and then ask ourselves, "where did that come from?" We act automatically without the slightest idea why we chose to react the way we did. We blame it on the weather, our physical condition, or on the other person. What we don't do is analyse our internal fabric in order to assess what makes us tick and why we act the way we do.

(2)   **Building a bridge between our logic and our emotions.** Self-management disciplines us to delay immediate action until we have information, and have taken enough time to think through the issue in order to prepare an appropriate response. When action is necessary, you can easily call upon your self-discipline to allow you time to gather yourself, to probe for details before becoming emotional, and then decide to act honestly and with dignity. Self-management teaches us self-control. For example, in the previous scenario, the husband could have used his self-discipline to walk up to his wife and friend, and ask why they were having lunch, in order to try and figure out what was going on. Or, he could have left the restaurant making a mental note to be more observant and watch for further clues to assist him in understanding the situation clearer. He would have later found to his delight that they had surprised him with a wonderful party and that was the reason for the PTA excuse and the lunch. If they had been having an affair, he would have had more data with which to confront them.

(3)   **Recognizing that we have the internal power to decide** how something or someone is going to affect us, the authority to choose

our own response, and the capability to take charge of our lives. When we internalize that:

★ we are not victims who have to allow others to dictate our thinking and emotions

★ the decisions we make depend on how we wish to direct our actions, which should not be based on the orders of others, we will then be able to view our possibilities in a more optimistic light

So often we become intense as we maintain a self-defeatist attitude, making it difficult to see our way clear of our immediate failure or spot a potential solution. When we remove this mental disposition and realize we have independent will, it can liberate us to make better decisions. In life's circumstances we may find that we have lost some of our personal liberties, but this does not mean that we have to lose our freedom to decide what will influence our thinking and what will not. Some prisoners of war have learned this first-hand as they utilized their ability to retain their mental freedom to internalize what they chose to and used their choice to create a focus of their own.

While living in Papua New Guinea I was faced with the realization that safety issues warranted me to remain indoors at night and prohibited my freedom to go outside at any given time. To some this was a major infraction on their lives. I decided to use this time of physical restrictions to write a book and to further increase my knowledge. I relished the opportunity of self-reflection and building a healthier me. Others used this situation to become angry, disillusioned and bored. We have the choice to redirect our emotional response to a more optimistic one.

(4)   **Using our self-awareness, creativity, and imagination to envision a better way.** Aside from having an independent will that gives us the capability to take action, we also have the authority to analyse our own thought processes and to evaluate our deeds. In doing so, we can design personal innovations which can make significant changes in our lives and in the lives of those around us. These resources can be used when dealing with adversity, in planning our course of action, and in creating a better life for ourselves. Unfortunately some of us become consumed and overwhelmed by our challenges. It necessitates discipline and courage to take charge of ourselves and find ways to better deal with our challenges.

Five-Step Reaction Strategy of Self-Management

The ability to readily identify our internal feelings, to acknowledge where they come from, while determining their validity, is necessary in formulating a plan on how to deal with them. This may sound like a long procedure, but you can become quite adept at going through this process quickly by using a *Five-Step Reaction Strategy*. The steps are:

1.   Relax

When dealing with someone who bothers us it is important to recognize that our bodies react according to our emotional response. Imagine if you were asked to speak before a group without having an opportunity to prepare yourself. For a few, this may be easy, but for the rest of us it is uncomfortable. Your internal voice says, "I am not ready... I will look like a fool… what will I say… oh no, how did this happen to me…" It will trigger your body to respond in physical ways. Your breathing can be shortened, you may notice that your hands are moist and may even shake, and you fear your smile may break if you have to move your mouth suddenly. This also occurs in times of danger and when faced with people who in some way have control over your emotions. Since we all react to negative stimuli in different ways, the best place to start is to relax. Take deep breaths through your nose, hold them for a second, and let them slowly out through your mouth. This can be done quickly and unnoticed. Another critical relaxation technique is to say to yourself, "I can handle this person (or situation), I am a bright and a strong individual, and I must relax and not let myself get stressed." By giving yourself encouragement you will begin to feel calmer and your body will start to relax.

2. Identify Your Emotions

One way we mismanage ourselves is by not identifying the underlining reasons why we feel the way we do. We can usually identify when we are hurt, angry, or afraid. These emotions serve to intensify our reaction but they don't necessarily help us deal with it. In order to know how to solve an internal issue we first have to understand why we feel the way we do.

3. Self-Control

Self-control is the result of blending:

(1)   character (represented by principles and values)

(2)   paradigms (the way we see)

(3)   self-awareness (which enables us to examine our own thoughts and the way we feel about ourselves and others (emotions))

(4)   creativity for imagining different ways to look at something

(5)   conscience (which defines what is right and what is wrong)

SELF-CONTROL

character	paradigms	self-awareness	creativity	conscience
principles values	maps analysis	thoughts	imagination	truth

Exercise

As you read the next story think about how you could blend your character, paradigms, self-awareness, creativity, and conscience to enable you to have self-control to deal with challenges and conflicts.

Donna was second-in-command of a progressive advertising agency. She worked directly under the authority of Margaret who was known and respected for her self-confidence, shrewdness, and unbending personality. She was a boss who knew what she wanted and got it in any manner that suited her needs. She knew how to charm clients into doing what she wanted and used intimidation tactics to maintain a high level of professionalism among her staff. Clients admired her for her skills and she was feared by her subordinates. Margaret became ill suddenly and had to have an operation which required several months of recuperation. This instantly took Donna out of the shadows and into the spotlight as the agency leader. There were two major client issues which Margaret had been addressing very guardedly prior to her illness and now demanded Donna's immediate attention. By contrast to Margaret, Donna was an unknown quantity and largely seen as a second banana who took care of Margaret's details. What the clients and staff had failed to recognize in their preoccupation with Margaret's persona was that Donna was the glue that kept the agency together. The clients and employees were fearful whether Donna could fill Margaret's shoes and problems were mounting out of their uncertainties.

Hint: Donna gave Margaret many of her ideas and learned to remain in the background because Margaret preferred to represent the company as a one-woman show. Donna had a strong character and believed in doing the right thing. She never fought for the limelight or struggled with Margaret over who would be perceived as the important one. Donna's goal was to be the best and to work on making the agency better as a result. But once she was thrust into the head role, she began to harness the reins of leadership in an effort to make things run more smoothly if not better.

Stop here and write down what you would do in Donna's place:

_____

_____

_____

_____

_____

_____

_____

What Donna Did

1. The first thing she did was call a meeting with all staff to officially let them know that no one was taking Margaret's place, instead she was filling a void and the excellence that Margaret expected was to be an ongoing mission for the group.

2. She then reviewed the challenges ahead and asked each department to meet individually to come up with a plan to address the problems facing their two major clients, and how they could maintain the quality service for their other clients.

3. Next, she asked the clerical team who were present at the meeting for the first time ever to design a plan on how to make the office more efficient, clients better treated, and technical work completed more effectively.

4. Donna also praised the staff for all the hard work they had done in the past and emphasized the important role of every employee. She told them of her open door policy and that no idea was too small to be perceived as insignificant.

5. She explained her style (which was opposite to Margaret), the issues she was faced with and asked for their support which she would in turn give to each of them. Donna asked the staff to meet in two days, decide who would give the departmental report, and to make sure everyone had an opportunity to give input. The charge to the employees was set.

6. She then called a meeting with the clients for the end of the next week during which she would present a strategy for dealing with their concerns. A special meeting with the major clients was

scheduled to present an update on their advertising campaigns. The purpose of the session was to immediately create continuity, to build trust and confidence that their work would still be achieved despite Margaret's absence. Donna knew that to delay these meetings would allow the rumour-mill to flourish and make her job harder.

CONSEQUENCES

1.   What was once perceived as a one-woman show became a total production with everyone newly energized and excited to be a part of making their company better. The office became a stimulating place where everyone began to share with each other and several staff communicating for the first time.

2.   The synergy was electrifying and no one person dominated. Donna made sure to drop in on meetings to observe and offer encouragement.

3.   When Donna arrived at the staff meeting, she was amazed that almost everyone was present and busily hanging charts, displays, and placing materials around the tables. She was excited by the enthusiasm of all of the staff who had worked overtime without being asked to complete their assignments.

4.   Donna made a few opening comments, then turned the meeting over to the departments and everyone from the creative team, mailroom, and secretarial pool to management, and the ad assistants gave creative and excellent presentations on how to better provide service as well as some very innovative ideas on how to solve their major clients' immediate concerns.

5. Donna and the other executives were delighted with the creativity, initiative and dedication of the staff and she thanked them for making this company better on behalf of Margaret, herself, and the other members of the executive team. She promised to incorporate their hard work into the proposal she and the other managers would be working on over the weekend.

6. Donna kept her promise and laboured over the development of a total advertising campaign. They managed to use everyone's ideas and each person in some way was reflected in the overall program.

7. The next week as promised, she presented their collective work. The staff lit up as they recognized a part of themselves in the proposal and everyone worked tirelessly and without additional pay to see it accomplished.

8. The clients were all impressed with the fresh approach and the comprehensive plan. They gave their approval and felt reassured that their goals would be achieved. In fact one client suggested Margaret should take an extended leave as things were more open and stimulating with new faces being exposed.

9. When Margaret returned to the office she was amazed at the vitality, confidence and openness of the staff. When she learned what took place and the enthusiasm of her clients she decided not to fix what had been repaired. She kept things as they stood and actually enjoyed having some of the pressure taken off of her shoulders.

10. Donna is no longer in the shadows, she is now an equal team member with Margaret. The two are now building a successful business. Donna had the strength of character to want to build

others while she evolved herself. She saw her employees as bright individuals with a potential to contribute more to the agency. Her self-awareness gave her insight into reaching higher professional levels.

Analysis

1.   Donna had the conscience and integrity not to try and overthrow Margaret's position, but to build upon it whereby everyone would win. She used her creative talents to try something new and involved everyone in the process. Her ability to blend her emotional and thinking minds provided a combination of heart and head in leadership which brought her respect and admiration.

2.   To Margaret's credit, she was able to let go and embrace the hard work and benefits that Donna achieved in her absence. She rewarded Donna by giving her a prominent role in the company.

Write down a situation which you were involved in or one you will need to deal with and describe how you did or will use your character, paradigms, self-awareness, creativity and conscience to deal with it.

_____

_____

_____

_____

_____

_____

_____

Learning to Feel Our Emotions

Learning the difference between feeling and being out of control is an important distinction. If someone you love passes away and you break down and cry, this is not losing control. This is showing real emotion and makes us compassionate and authentic. Allowing yourself to express pain, fear, frustration, or anger is not being out of control, unless you vent it in self-destructing ways that hurt yourself or other people. The man in the restaurant illustration was out of control because he vented his jealousy and anger on his wife and friend without giving them the option of explaining.

Expressing how you feel and showing your emotions in a non-threatening way is different from projecting your feelings onto someone and making them share in your emotional episode. When the man verbally abused his wife and friend he made them a party to his emotions without giving them a choice as to whether they wanted to participate. The man who expresses emotion over the loss of a loved one is showing his emotion, and not making others participate in his grief. If they become involved, it's because they choose to console him or share in the loss. There is a difference between personal expression of emotion and outburst of emotion that is not personal because it involves other people in the act or the feeling itself. I recall a woman who lost her child in a car accident. Distraught, she went to a bar to drink then started a fight with another woman for no apparent reason. She was angry and guilt-ridden and wanted someone to participate in her grief. She chose this unproductive way which resulted in her arrest.

After the episode she sought counselling and hopefully she has now learned to share her personal expression of grief with someone who can help her. Having control is an important goal in self-management. It takes disciplining our mind and taking the moment between the stimulus (what happens), and our response (how we will act) to think about the best way to deal with a person or an event. It is in this time-frame that we can discipline ourselves to be either productive or unproductive.

4. Be Forthright

Once we decide to take a stand on an issue, it is then important to determine our response. So often we decide on a course of action that we don't follow through. We either procrastinate or let our fears prevent us from saying and doing what we know is right. For example, if I had not been forthright in letting the woman in the grocery store know that I was not going to participate in gossip, I would have been faced with the same situation over and over again. Prior to that encounter, I was not direct with her, I would smile and not say anything only to stew over her comments or complain to my husband all week which drove him crazy. Finally, I knew I needed to be forthright. The manner in which you approach someone is as important as what you say. Giving mixed messages can be counterproductive to what we had hoped to accomplish. If you say things without being forthright, and without taking into consideration the dignity of the other person then you may be subject to more controversy there than was in the first place. Sarcasm or cruel remarks never solve a problem they only intensify it.

However no matter how honest and direct you are there are some people who will refuse to get the point, or use your sincerity against you. These people are devious in their desire to understand your concerns, and when they ask you what they did to hurt your feelings, and you tell them openly, they try and make you feel badly by placing the blame on you by saying things like: "you are overly sensitive", "how could you say that?", or "if you had acted differently, I would have responded to you in a more positive way". For the most part, when others do not take any responsibility for their actions it usually means that they prefer for you to admit a wrongdoing and change your opinions. They see it as a means of invalidating your own feelings. There may be other times when others will not work with you on solving an issue. This makes it impossible to get them to acknowledge another viewpoint. In this situation it is appropriate to stand by your decision and be consistent, concise, and in control.

5. Feel Positive

When we have to face someone or something that is a problem sometimes we do so in a negative or dreadful way. In resolving a dilemma, we either go in with a fighting spirit, a defeatist attitude, or we hate the idea of having to be faced with the conflict in the first place. Having to deal with uncomfortable situations is a fact of life. It is difficult to go for long periods of time without being involved in some degree with a stressful situation. Being positive means that you are looking for a win/win possibility and an opportunity that would facilitate growth. We must learn to maintain an air of optimism, a respect for our own capabilities, and help others realize their own.

If we believe in our own strength and power, it should set us free to be co-operative and willing to work with others. Being positive should be a complement to being realistic. If you find something is out of your control or someone just doesn't like you no matter what you try to do differently, still be positive by not taking it personally. They have a right not to like you or agree with you and you have the right not to let it affect you. Positive people say: "let's do it, we can, I will, I understand, I take responsibility for my actions, I will change and I know there is a better way".

By contrast negative people say things like: "we can't do it, I can't, you don't understand, it isn't my responsibility, I see no need to change, there is no other way". Enthusiasm is contagious, so is pessimism. But only one is progressive.

The philosophy of self-management is to simply know who you are, what you feel, what you stand for, and how you want to conduct yourself. Self-management does not imply you are not yourself, or that you are a cold and controlled robot. It does mean owning your own thought processes; choosing the way you want to think and feel. It makes those unimportant things less important, and gives you the wisdom to sort out what is truly useful to you from what is not. Self-management is the positive bridge between emotion and logic. When you don't manage yourself, any idea, opinion, or unsubstantiated viewpoint can leave you emotionally running in all directions, and causing you to have temper tantrums, or other unhelpful behaviours that in retrospect were not necessary. This is why some people spend so much time apologizing and putting out fires for things they said or have done. Self-management provides a screening mechanism for handling all of the stimuli we receive. It organizes what we internalize, and how we address the information. We also have a filtering system for when we have internalized an issue or response, felt it, dealt with it, and then let it go. Too much unnecessary input can cloud our internal core and make it more difficult to reach our productive qualities for personal success.

Inner Organizational Tools

Without effective instruments our precision is weakened.

When faced with adversity, turmoil, or uncertainty we have inner tools that can help us deal with a situation. These resources can sharpen our focus and redirect our responses so that they are appropriate and representative of how we really feel. In order to use this edge, we must first know that it exists, that it is available upon command, and when it is best to use it. Inner tools are organized under four general categories:

(1) **Intuition.** This is our wisdom and keen insight. Think of the time when someone asked you to do them a favour and something inside you told you not to. Those who listen to their inner voice may have saved themselves from a negative situation. For others it may have resulted in a bad experience. By listening to our internal wisdom, mother wit or inner voice, we are validating the intuition we were born with. Haven't you heard people say: "something

inside warned me of this (or from doing that)". Listen and respond. The good advice you give to others, and the good judgement you use when taking care of someone else are the same insights you should use for yourself. It works, if we use it.

(2)   **Logic and analysis** is our ability to look at the whole picture, breaking it down into its parts and from there we are able to solve a problem. How many times do we just pick up one detail and run with it as we would take one bite of a sandwich before we dash off to an appointment. We have an innate ability to think through a problem and analyse its parts in order to come to a conclusion. Some people are better at doing this than others. They take the time and energy to use the process of looking at the whole and then the sum parts. Some of us tend to use generalizations, stereotypes, symbolism, and other one-dimensional indicators to make our assumptions. The detective in us is hidden when we are faced with having to make decisions. We look instead to the fastest way to rid ourselves of having to make the decision by relying on others, or opt for a quick-fix remedy that has no real substance.

　　The gift of logic and analysis (L.A.) is one that needs to be developed, nurtured, and encouraged. Isn't it ironic that many of us have this skill but we turn it on and off like a water facet? We use it in professional settings or when helping others, but when we need it in personal or social situations we let it lay dormant. The skill of seeing the whole and its sum parts is a process that we can use in every situation in life. The man in the story who saw his wife eating lunch with his friend did not use it and others who are faced with personal and career challenges often forget it. The L.A. process of decision-making involves three steps:

★   *Looking at the whole deck of cards.* If we are expected to play a game of cards it would be wise to first know whether we are being dealt from a full deck, what cards we have in our hand, and what cards are in the hands of others. By knowing this we will be in a better position to analyse the kind of game others are playing and what cards we would need to make an appropriate call. Sometimes it is impossible to know the full deck and we have to rely on our intuition and skill to make the proper decision, and sometimes we may not succeed. The important point to remember is that knowledge is power and power should be the opportunity to do what is right.

★ *Categorizing the information you receive.* When the data pool starts flooding you need to place things in sections, organizing what is the most necessary and what is the least. For example, use sections of: fact, fiction, important, unimportant, potential consideration, and as-need-be basis. Then move on to prioritizing the categories and deciding how you will address the issues and the possible results of doing so. Proceed to place the issues you are faced with under the appropriate section. This will give you an opportunity to think through the issue and sift through the details that are not vital to forming a position.

★ *Understanding the environmental climate.* Once the information is organized and concise, it is now important to know the backdrop upon which you will be making your decision or taking action. The best laid plans can fall flat if you neglect to know who you are dealing with, the political ramifications of what you are doing, and the general atmosphere of a situation or event. Walking into a meeting to give a presentation on the dangers of cigarette smoking to a smokers rights activist group would not be productive unless you knew going in that the group holds this viewpoint and your speaking presentation takes this into account.

(3)   **Imagination and creativity.** These provide ways we can envision a better way of solving a problem or make a better life for ourselves and others. One of the most stimulating and exciting inner tools we possess is the ability to use our imagination to draw a picture of what we see for ourselves and the world and to be able to step as close as we can to what it would be like to be someone or something else. Without this ability we would only be as functional as our own experiences would entail, limiting us to a more narrow perspective of a life full of differences and specialities. Imagination gives us an opportunity to transform situations into workable and important innovations for the betterment of humankind or our own lives. Like anything good or bad, the first place it starts is in our imagination. If you never imagine yourself with an education, or a position of leadership, then the chances of your seeking or taking advantage of these opportunities are lessened. Our imagination can also be an escape mechanism to help us deal with loneliness, boredom, a bad situation, unhappiness, and in the case of prisoners of war or any kind of incarceration, a release from the anxiety of a given situation or environment. It allows us to create a place where we would find peace and lets us envision ourselves as we would like to be. Our creativity is an extension of our imagination and can put into focus a way to obtain our vision or find an avenue for developing a new and fresh perspective in solving an old burdensome problem. It unleashes our authenticity and talents for building something that is unique and which represents our own self-expression.

(4)   **Emotion.** This refers to a feeling and its particular thoughts, psychological and biological states, and range of tendency to act. They are our conscious reaction to the things that happen to us. Emotions can serve as a reminder that we are loving, caring, and feeling members of the universe. They allow us to express ourselves

and provide a release as we go through the human experience. Our emotions can be positive or negative depending on our understanding of our moods, temperament, and the signals that call us to action.

Emotional signals include: anger, sorrow, fear, empathy, sentiment, joy, pride, sadness, enjoyment, love, surprise, guilt, caring, hate, frustration, and laughter. Imagine if the world were devoid of emotion, where everyone was indifferent and apathetic toward one another, or if no one felt anything or showed any reaction to what we said or did. We would all just walk around talking with no one expressing feelings, and all we would receive is more dialogue. Have you ever been excited about something that you felt was good for you only to have the person you shared your news with look at you with no emotion or positive feedback? Do you remember the time when you told of your good fortune only to have others say the right things, but their reaction or lack of emotion said another? This probably left you feeling flat, if not frustrated by the lack of interest shown.

The area of emotion has received a lot of attention and people have joked about women being emotional and men unemotional. In relationships couples argue about the lack of emotional support. The flip side of emotion is when people are accused of being too sensitive, too angry, or too frustrated. Some people even accuse one another of taking everything as a laughing matter. The problem is not one of lack of emotion, it is one of balance, and more importantly, the lack of self-control. In today's world, many of us are out of control. Instead of resolving conflict by seeking a win/win result through non-threatening discussion we see people fighting, or worse, killing one another.

Rudeness, meanness, and impatience mark our society. How many people do you see with smiles on their faces as you walk in the streets of our cities? How many people receive or give compliments in a day? How many people care about others in their schools or work? How many people really feel for someone else's plight? Unfortunately not too many. We have become driven by money, power, and self-gain. We have become obsessed with obtaining the best of material things as our life's goal. Seeking to acquire a comfortable lifestyle and to have the respect of others in and of itself is not the problem. It is the way in which we go about it. We cheat, mistreat one another, manipulate, power play, steal and even kill as if it were a right. I recall a young man who told me that the key to life is not right but might. The fiercest and strongest shall dominate and control. This mindset does not make great leaders or great people; it only yields tyrants. Greatness is derived by the self-discipline to achieve a goal using compassion which will make a contribution to the well-being of people. If we are always emotional and find it impossible to laugh at ourselves, we may need to create a balance by adding more humour in our lives. If the reverse is true, we may need to tap emotions that give us a broader range of expression. Balancing our emotional mind with our thinking mind will permit us to be more real and honest to ourselves and others. It would help us give of ourselves and add depth to our character. Some of us choose to block out certain emotions to protect ourselves from hurt, while others use the power of feeling to control and dominate. In many instances individuals have spent more time on developing their logic side while neglecting the emotional and feeling part of their being.

Whatever path you have selected to direct your emotions it is critical that you learn to use the richness of expression that is yours and balance it with your wealth of feeling. If you are angry, sometimes it is productive to show that side as it clears the air and gives you an opportunity to share your disappointment or disapproval as long as it is not threatening the well-being of others. Physical violence is never acceptable in any situation other than self-defence. Our emotions are one of the most important, yet most misused and misunderstood resources that we have. Using our emotions can bring clarity to who we are, define us, help us give and receive love, strength, empowerment and respect. In essence it is the basic foundation for making us human.

Five-Step Self-Management Process

This five-step technique is designed to assist you in dealing with the internal and external challenges you face. This self-management process will also help you better manage your inner resource tools.

Sharon, a friend of mine, was extremely jealous. Every time her husband looked at another woman she became angry and at some point took it out on him. What resulted were arguments leaving both parties feeling miserable. Her behaviour was destroying their marriage. To deal with feelings of jealousy and other destructive behaviours which can undermine your self-esteem and relationships, there are five steps you can take. They will help you deal with self-defeating attitudes which prevent you from feeling inner freedom and harmony.

1. Awareness

The first step in dealing with a problem is to recognize that it exists. So often, we stay in denial and do not admit there is a problem or, most importantly, that we are the faced with the problem. Even if you did not initiate the issue it may still affect you if it involves someone close to you. In Sharon's case she felt guilty for feeling insecure and treating her husband badly. This feeling of guilt resulted in a spiral effect where she became self-critical and tried to avoid the anxiety of being responsible for any trouble in her marriage by blaming her husband and any woman he admired.

Perhaps, if she had acknowledged her jealousy and admitted that the emotion she felt was due to the fear that she might not measure up, she would have been on the road to healing her insecurity. The real problem was her low self-esteem. Her jealousy was a manifestation of her negative belief system. Because of her fear she hurt herself which resulted in pain and anxiety.

The awareness stage should begin to create a need to work on a resolution with the help of a trusted friend, a loved one, or a professional counsellor. By acknowledging a problem you have made an important step toward growth. The awareness stage is used in many self-help programs of recovery. Once you have made this important discovery you are then ready for the analysis step.

2. Analysis

It is one thing to say I have a problem with jealousy, prejudice, self-dislike, an inability to connect with someone at a deeper level, or any other issue that affects you internally. However, it's another to try and sort out the who, what, when and why. Let's use Sharon's problem of jealousy as an example of dealing with the analysis stage. Sharon should begin to think about why she feels this way, who or what triggers this response, what self-talk does she use during the development of her behaviour, when is she most vulnerable, and why does her fear or anger build to the point where she reacts in a negative manner. She may want to delve into her background to determine what she was told about herself and what is her self-image as a result. By doing this exploration she can find the source of her behaviour. Sharon realized her actions were not her authentic self because of the guilt she felt after each episode. It may be helpful to analyse a personal issue with a trained specialist or trusted friend who may provide unbiased and helpful input. In any case it is important to always use the analysis step as a means of bringing clarification and understanding, as opposed to condemning yourself or others for a problem. It is important to be honest and positive in your assessment with the goal of becoming a better you. Once you uncover the source of the problem then you must determine the inner challenge.

3. INNER COMMITMENT TO THE CHALLENGE

Often we think we can just will a bad habit or feeling away. It may work for some very determined few but for most of us it takes a consistent, focused, and dedicated effort to change our way of thinking and acting. This step requires the realization of what needs to be changed, what it will take to make the necessary alterations in our life, and the acknowledgement of the degree of commitment important to meeting the demands of the challenge. Being aware of the importance of daily affirmations is a start in focusing your mind on the ways that you need to self-direct your thinking. Affirmations can be a positive alternative to the negative scenario you play out in your mind when fearful or faced with a challenge. Affirmations should be positive and real written or mental statements you make about yourself. It is especially useful to use affirmations or positive self-talk when faced with a situation that is threatening. Sharon's affirmations for dealing with jealousy could be: "I know I am feeling insecure due to my lack of self-esteem, I must remember that I am a beautiful and valuable person who needs to trust the love of my husband and above all love myself. I must not let my fears or uncertainties about myself build stories in my mind that may not be real and that put me down."

It is helpful to read inspirational materials to nourish the mind with positive and healthy thoughts about ourselves. You have already started this activity by reading this book. Making affirmations each day will train your mind to think positive thoughts and stop the onslaught of negative ones that have become a habit. Say to yourself: "I will accept my talents and learn to let my love inside fill me with peace and appreciation for who and what I am. I will learn to accept the gifts that others have as well as the ones that I have been blessed with and I will not compete or compare with others as a means of determining my own self-worth." Prayer is another form of affirmation and releases the self-defeating inner voice that wants to pull you down instead of bring you up. Prayer affirms your unity with God and gives you strength and a renewed sense of purpose which can lead to creativity. Other daily affirmations are, for example: "I will allow myself to make mistakes, while at the same time, I will give myself permission to keep trying, I am a loveable and valuable person." It is also helpful to ask others you trust to help you in dealing with your challenge and to give you encouragement and praise. When you have made the commitment and realized the challenge the next step is to design the strategy.

4. STRATEGY

Most successful ventures, whether it's a business merger, a skill you want to learn, or a basketball team attempting to win the finals, begin by first establishing a goal and then a strategy. By doing this, you can start developing a plan of action taking into account your strengths, weaknesses, and the environmental issues that must be considered. From this research, a detailed outline will emerge of the course you will need to develop to achieve your goals. The first place to start in designing your personal strategy is to establish overall goals and each week design objectives which will move you closer to meeting your goals.

If you want to start speaking up for the things you want instead of not saying anything and spending hours of anguish because you are shy about expressing yourself, begin writing down your goal(s) which could be, for example:

★ *The first strategy:* your objective or goal: to become more assertive in expressing my opinion.

★ *The second strategy:* to determine what speaking format intimidates you most. Next, you would begin to practice in this format while finding tools that would help you most.

★ *The third strategy:* to define what would be the most effective communication style which would empower me when speaking or writing in this situation, and then practice in front of a mirror, behind a podium, or when in a meeting-style format.

If you are using writing as a means of expression, it is useful to learn the various writing techniques that are used to persuade, inform, and debate. Related materials are numerous and can be found in the library or bookstore. This activity would provide a great opportunity to involve your mentor or friend in playing the role of the listener or reader.

Another objective might be: *to find additional resources to help me maintain my goal.* If you are expected to present your ideas verbally you may want to develop a point outline which would flesh out exactly what message you would bring to a discussion. Remember, practice makes perfect.

The more you actually do something you fear, whether it's public speaking or expressing a dislike for poor service in a restaurant or giving praise to others when appropriate, the better you will become at expressing your true feelings. Practising in everyday life the skills you want to enhance, will make it easier to overcome your fears when under pressure or during important occasions.

Strategy implies action and to achieve any goal, whether personal, or professional means doing. For instance, when the alarm clock goes off early in the morning–get up fast and go. The strategy-step is the action part of your program for self-improvement and should always be followed by the final step, evaluation.

5. Evaluation

If we rely on the authentic inner voice that roots for our well-being and knows our true greatness, and not the self-containment voice which wants us to stay the same, and undermines our effort to grow by reminding us of all the negative aspects of our being, we can usually correctly assess when we have succeeded or failed. When we use the self-containment voice that wants to hold us back, we become our own worst critic. We analyse to a fault everything we ever attempt to do. We never let anything slip by. We find errors even if we have to dig deep. When everyone praises us, we refuse to accept their remarks by highlighting any mistake we made, no matter how minor.

I coached a colleague of mine on preparing a speech. I was very impressed with the way she delivered the speech and with its content. In fact she gave a terrific presentation. However, she made one mistake in a text of many pages and consequently dwelled on that one small part. Because of this error, she missed the joy of the applause and the many accolades that followed. It was almost as if she couldn't bear to admit that she had a speaking talent which would somehow prove her self-containment voice wrong in its assessment of her abilities. She complained about her momentary loss of thought and proceeded to paint the whole speech with the same negative brush. She didn't realize that she had the control to forgive herself for making a mistake and that she could also give herself permission to enjoy her success. She proceeded to bask in her security cocoon of being a perfectionist where she took pride in always trying to be perfect. Upon hearing her long and unfair analysis of her presentation, as her mentor and friend I finally said, "you did an excellent job, learn from your mistakes but give yourself praise when deserved, you think you have to be perfect, the fact is you are not perfect. No one else is for that matter". I hoped that what I had said would shake her loose from this self-loathing posture. I intended my comments to be instructive. Yet I could not determine if I had gone too far. After she had time to think, I received a call from her asking me if I would work with her again on another presentation. To my surprise and excitement, she began to take charge of her work. When she gave her speech she still had a tendency to be over-critical of herself but I noticed that she now allowed herself to feel some of the rewards of her hard work. She still strived for improvement which was a more fair goal, but this time she approved of herself. As I saw her smile and genuinely embrace the applause, I stood up and clapped, not only for the great job she had done, but for the fact that she was now beginning to appreciate herself. She later told me that she was always haunted by a need to be perfect. She used an imaginary measure that originated from her need to be accepted and to convince her inner protagonist that she was a person of talent and worth.

It had been a composite of many ideas my friend had received over the years which set conditions on whether she could accept praise and love. The stress from trying to earn love which was conditional, caused her to doubt the instances when she did receive positive recognition and acceptance. She had formed a self-containment voice which made her goal that of perfection, which was an illusion to cover up the fact that she was afraid that when she did reach a point of perfection she would still not be loved. So the quest became more comfortable than the actual achievement of excellence, and facing the possibility of still being hurt by a lack of love and acceptance.

So often we are unfair to ourselves because of some imaginary measure that originated from our need to be accepted. We find it hard to convince our inner self we are a person of talent and worth. As we process the many ideas we have received about ourselves over the years, our voice of containment reinforces the ideas of imperfection.

As we struggle to prove our inner voices right we cause conflict within ourselves when we receive positive information. While some of us are too hard on ourselves and strive for perfection others never take responsibility for their actions and always point the finger elsewhere as the cause of their own problems. Usually these people have a low self-esteem which makes them unwilling to see the reality of their actions. It is also painful for them to face the real reasons why they have become people who hurt others. It is easier to pretend to be a nice person and make excuses when your actions do not match. Blaming others rather than taking responsibility for unkind deeds is a clever way of avoiding the need to change. Seeking the evaluation of others is important to self-development. We can learn lessons from everyone. It is the people who hurt us who often teach us the most. By accepting positive criticism, and internalizing only those comments that help us grow while forgetting the ones that are spiteful or counterproductive we will enrich our internal being.

PART FOUR

EQ WORKPLACE SKILLS

The M.E.N.E.M. Secret

M.E.N.E.M. (Mind, Eyes, Nose, Ears, Mouth.) There is nothing more exciting then the collaboration of all of one's senses.

Have you ever been in a situation that started out as a problem, but by the time you internalized and dissected the issues and put your perspective on it, everything suddenly became chaotic, confused, and out of control? To add to your troubles, you then find yourself in quicksand which is taking you under inch by inch. Even though there is a sturdy branch right next to your stronger arm you are still unable to grab it and pull yourself out. It's like there is a heavy weight keeping you down. The weight is your vast internal opinionates all trying to get your attention, and struggling to tell you what to do and how to think. It's those many interpreters defining for you what everything and everybody means in your external world that are all working for you, but not with you which are the reasons for the mismanagement. We can use our inner opinionates to tell us how to analyse a situation. However the problem is we have not trained them to filter through our past insecurities, hurt and biases, or to define our problems, what we need in order to be effective, and the best course to take for finding happiness and fulfilment.

Our inner opinionates are usually free to run in all directions collecting and sorting data, yet we haven't the foggiest idea as to what to do with the information during a problem or crisis. When we do decide what to do it's usually based on disconnected or irrational data which fails to give us a rounded picture. We use old film to take new pictures which causes a double exposure and blurred image. Past experience is important when combined with new openness. Opinionates even run rampant during calm and happy times. They interface within our senses: our eyes (what we see), our ears, (what we hear), our mind (what we think), our mouths (what we say), and our nose (what we smell or sense). But we usually do not organize their work or give them direction as to their mission. As a result they fail to work together for our best interest.

The M.E.N.E.N Secret is simply a collaborative strategy for using all of our senses when making decisions. It provides us with a framework for sustaining an internal management system. The secret is a process to help us to grasp the total picture, using details as a stepping-stone to understanding and managing our emotions in concert with our rational mind, so that we will utilize the best alternatives. Each of our senses plays a role in helping us unravel the complex situations we face.

1. Mind: What We Think About Ourselves can Either Increase or Decrease Our Potential

The depth and capacity of the human mind is startling. The average person uses only a tiny portion of their mental capabilities. We have the ability to feed our minds with stimulating information which can expand and enrich its base of knowledge. When we fill it with positive and productive thoughts we allow it to move in a direction that is encouraging and fulfilling.

Our mind can play back for us anything we suggest to it. It will sort through the best and worst to give us a perspective that works if we only teach it to do so. This takes mental discipline, study, creativity, and the courage to try new and innovative challenges to increase our body of knowledge. Reading, listening to experts, and experiencing new things will broaden our horizons and prepare us to be a student of life as opposed to a dropout. The United Negro College Fund motto is: "A mind is a terrible thing to waste". This is true in decision-making as well as in daily life. The seeds we plant in our mind can either grow flowers or weeds. It is up to us to use this magnificent tool which is fundamental to our progress.

Negative thinking can hinder our self-development: Our most important critic lies within our minds and can be our worst foe. The world we live in encourages us to view ourselves as inferior and as needing things we do not have. We are conditioned to think of the negative instead of the positive largely because it benefits other people and puts the emotional ball in our court and not in the court of those who are trying to maintain their edge. By allowing these negative influences to become a part of our thinking and perception of ourselves we give others control over what we think and what we do. Self-defeating thinking limits our ability to ask for help when needed and it creates a false pride which becomes a source of oppression when it prevents us from doing the things necessary to find inner peace, happiness, and fulfilment.

2. Eyes: They Can Bring Clarity and Focus to a Situation

Another M.E.N.E.M. secret component is to use our eyes to observe what is around us. We have the opportunity to look at events, people, and details in a way that can add a dimension to our understanding that is imperative in decision-making. There is a whole field in non-verbal communication which says basically that looking at how someone acts, their body movements, their facial expressions and even their eyes can tell you more than what they say. There are courses to help you become more alert in observing people or situations. Many professions require a person to be observant using their eyes to assess people, and places. Police officers, doctors and scientists, are a few examples of jobs where seeing and observing plays an important role.

A friend of mine who is a nurse came to visit me. Although she hadn't seen me in two years I was impressed that she remembered even small details I had changed in my living-room and incidental item I had added. When I complimented her on this talent she told me that as a nurse she was trained to notice and evaluate the patient for every detail. In doing so she sharpened her eye for detail and memory.

How many of us go to and from work and never notice the environment around us? We limit the opportunity to enjoy the beauty of life. This lack of notice can also be dangerous if we are unaware of the elements that can hurt us. Children are prone to become so absorbed with what they are doing that they fail to see a potential car approaching or an unknown individual coming too close to them.

To train the use of our eyes as a means of gathering additional information is one of the best investments we can make in becoming more aware. It is critical in every aspect of life. In negotiations watching body movements can be enlightening. By looking at someone's eyes you can often tell whether or not they have a winning hand at cards, if their smile is sincere, and if they are angry, the intensity. Seeing your world, knowing the changes around you and what seems to stay the same will be increasingly necessary as you interact with a multitude of stimuli. Eyes can provide a two-way mirror as you use them to view the world, they can also reveal your inner thinking.

3. Nose: Like an Alarm, it Senses the Good and the Bad

Our sense of smell is something we often take for granted. We use it mostly unconsciously unless we smell smoke which triggers our awareness to the potential of a fire, or when we smell something foul which indicates we must investigate further, or when we detect something is spoiled, thus saving us from eating contaminated food. The scent of a rose or perfume is pleasing to most and can mean something special. To others the smell of rain or the earth brings a feeling of serenity and peace. Allowing our nose to add to our other senses gives us completeness. To experience life is to take in all of its aromas. For those of us unable to see, the use of our sense of smell is invaluable. Through using our nose more some of us are able to sense unspoken tension as the body expels odours that signal various emotional and physical conditions. Animals have a keen sense of smell which tells them a lot about the world they are exploring.

One of the most vital aspects of our nose is the air we take into our lungs with it every day. It provides a lifeline which connects us to the atmosphere. When we are unable to breathe on our own it takes in the instrument that helps us to breathe. In sports and any exercise routine breathing through our nose can help sustain our activity. Yoga has a basis in breathing and the nose is fundamental to assisting in taking in new air and expelling the toxins that cause us distress. This is valuable when we are emotionally upset, nervous or unsettled. The saying "the nose knows" is true. What we smell in our surroundings can serve as a warning to be cautious or to leave. To smell the beauty of our environment is one of the joys we have. It warms us and summons all of our senses to partake in the pleasures of the scent. It can even be a team captain. What the nose smells will usually put the other senses into action.

4. EARS: THEY ALLOW US TO HEAR, BUT DO WE LISTEN?

Of all the communication skills that we could improve none is more critical than our ability to listen. It is easier to talk and more exciting to share what we know than to make the effort to understand another human being. The hardest activity is to listen to others and learn. Listening is a skill within itself. It can even be painful when confronted with a long-winded conservationist. Effective listening takes patience and a willingness to seek new information. To love is also to listen. We are conditioned to want to set the record straight, to tell our version, and to express ourselves in order to be understood. For the most part, we do not listen, and if we do it is to either prepare our response in order to validate our own thinking, to find a way to entrap another into saying what we want to hear, or wish to interpret what the speaker is really saying because in our minds we know best.

Our fast-paced society has no place for taking the time to hear what someone has to say. Everything is in a 30-second sound bite. If the message isn't made clear fast, the audience will dismiss you. We have grown accustomed to the action-packed movies of today where you hardly have time to sit down and take the first mouthful of popcorn before you are practically blown out of your seat by the action on the screen. If you stutter or talk slowly most people will finish their answer to your comment before you have had an opportunity to tell it. Women are famous for tapping into their emotions quickly and by the time their men have opened up to the point of saying: "I feel …" we have already told them the rest of how they feel, why they feel that way, how it makes us feel, the solution, and what we are going to have for dinner, all before he has had time to say how he feels. The tendency to hear while our mouths are going presents several problems; first, when we are talking chances are we are not thinking as much, observing as well, and learning what others think and feel. By not having enough input we are subject to making assumptions, being presumptuous and ill-advised in decision-making.

Listening can take many forms. We can listen with empathy (really identifying with the feelings, thoughts, and attitudes of another), for understanding (learning the depth and breadth of what another has said), to support (giving support when another must face a challenge or overcome adversity), to increase knowledge (improving our intellectual abilities), for truth (finding the reality of a situation), and sympathy (consoling another).

By listening we will not only gain understanding which will be useful in our daily life, we will also receive respect and admiration from others. There is nothing more significant to an individual then to be listened to and respected for their right to have opinion even if they do not agree with our own. Talking is important and is a skill we use every day in order to survive. Even if we do not talk with our voices we still talk by using sign language or other technology. There must be a balance between listening and talking which enables us to listen for understanding and to speak with intelligence.

5.   Mouth: What it Says can Define us Rightly or Wrongly

Remember the sayings: "if only I had thought before I spoke ... I put my foot in my mouth ... I was way ahead until I opened my mouth," and as a friend of mine says about her quick responses, "what comes up comes out." These adages represent the fact that what we say has tremendous impact on how we are perceived, whether we resolve a problem or fan it to new heights. Much of what we have and the consequences on our lives depends on what we say and how we say it. Some of us spend additional time cleaning up after our mouths have caused a misunderstanding or misrepresentation of what it is we had intended to say. Often we try and change what we have said to save a situation from becoming worse, or to protect an image we have created.

In relationships we say things to hurt, and to gain power over a conflict or a person. When using what we say as a instrument to control or make ourselves superior, it becomes a liability to our ability to our growth as a person, and to find meaningful and fulfilling associations. We have heard that how we look determines how attractive we are. It is also true that what we say can decide if we are attractive. Have you seen a physically beautiful person lose much of their allure the minute they open their mouth? It's like they are transformed right in front of your eyes. Some individuals who may not fit the standards of beauty, but once you listen to them speak, the quality of what they say, their humour and sensitivity shines through making them beautiful. If "the eyes are the gateway to your soul," then the mouth is the opening to your personality. It can define you in ways that are real, or in ways that distort who you really are.

Many times we have only one chance to say the right thing. The biggest problem with our mouth is that it is usually controlled by our emotions. It's like a domino effect, once the emotion is unleashed the mouth follows suit and starts verbalizing what is happening inside of us, and the outcome is one of venting our frustration. This may not be negative if the person who receives this outburst is a friend with understanding, or who has a vested interest in our success. It can, however, be harmful if it is done in an unfriendly and hostile environment. Our mouth and what we allow to come out of it tells something about us and whether what we have said has really represented who we are. It can also determine how others perceive us just from that one encounter.

While on vacation my tooth started bothering me. I made an appointment with a dentist who was recommended by the hotel concierge where I was staying. As I was sitting in the dentist's office waiting my turn, I heard a loud noise in the conference room. The doctor and his dental hygienist had gotten into a rip-roaring fight. She accused him of breaking his promise of leaving his wife. This fight went on for about ten minutes, and ended with the doctor slamming the door and going into his examining room. After what seemed like a half-hour the receptionist sheepishly told me I could go into the office. I thanked her and said I was cancelling this appointment. I went to another dentist that day. I was told later that the first dentist was the best, and would have done a great job. Nonetheless hearing the words and learning of the unprofessional way in which he conducted his office lowered his credibility in my mind. I was hesitant, because I didn't want someone working in my mouth in a state of frustration and anger.

Like the dentist, we sometimes let our mouths speak in ways that can hurt us. It is something we must attend to in a world that places much importance on the spoken word. Politicians know best about the influence words have on creating an image, giving authority, or taking it away, and how it can enhance our personality. A man who shouts at his children as a means of communicating may be a wonderful father but if what he says and how he says it comes across harshly, others will perceive him in a negative light. A woman who finds fault with everything and says so is not an individual others would like to invite to their party. What we say can give us credibility or expose us as frauds. Unfortunately, our society is overly impressed with an individual's propensity for using verbal communication to their advantage. We have seen talented speakers persuade many to follow their words to their advantage and not always for the betterment of others. These individuals may not have real depth or character but they have the words and the ability to translate emotion into language that fills up one's insecurities. The significance of what we say and how we say it should never be taken for granted.

Self-improvement in using our mouths to effectively represent us is a goal to maintain. We need to combine our minds with sensitivity, and a commitment to think before we speak, and to always keep in mind it isn't always what we say, it's how we say it. There are times when we must speak a truth which can hurt others, but if we treat others with dignity and say what is necessary with respect, that is the best we can do. The rest is up to the level of maturity of the other person receiving the information.

M.E.N.E.N. Collaboration

To put all of our senses together and working for us is one of the most powerful actions we can take. Imagine sitting in a confrontational meeting and using your mind to think about your strategy, your eyes to observe all around you, your mouth to say the things that effectively represent you which can promote a win/win outcome, your ears well trained to listen for the truth of the matter, and your nose helping to maintain your calmness, sensing your surroundings and the people there. What a formidable internal team you would have! The result would be your increased self-respect, self-authority, self-confidence, and above all the emotional maturity to recognize, appreciate and encourage the same qualities in others.

EQ Skills for Success in the Workplace

Working environments are going to run out of steam unless they start cultivating and applying EQ skills in the workplace. These skills are, but not limited to:

1. Delaying Gratification

One of the main reasons why people do not succeed and solve problem effectively is an inability to delay gratification and cope with the pain that is associated with dealing with conflict. The "party now and worry later" mentality affects many people. Delaying gratification also involves impulse-control. The suffering associated with problem-solving causes many people to avoid conflict to the point where there is a pile-up effect that intensifies the problem far beyond its original state.

The saying: "taking the line of least resistance," implies that an individual will do what is pleasurable and comfortable rather than what is needed and challenging and will make him grow. In a work environment where time is of the essence, the ability to tackle hard tasks in an expedient manner is most beneficial to reaching a goal. Procrastination is a by-product which leaves the individual and team at odds when dealing with time-frames.

2. Self-Discipline

Self-discipline is at the core of problem-solving and achieving success. Without the discipline to accept responsibility, to work toward what is right and just, and to balance our conflicting aspirations with the objectives of the work environment, we will find ourselves frustrated, unhappy, and unable to realize our goals. Being willing to stand in the gap between what is right and wrong until others address certain unfair issues is a personal leadership strength worth cultivating. In doing so, you need to be politically attuned and have learned the organizational expectations well while at the same time being capable of withstanding the pressure. The extent to which standing firm on our principles when they are being threatened or compromised is a measure of our discipline.

3. The Play of Communication

Think of a time when you were in a meeting or a situation which involved several people. You had to work together to achieve a goal. What appears to be an easy enough task turns into a big production. This production is caused by the underlining play that is being constructed and the roles that are taken by the members of the group. To go further with the play analogy you have a cast which is made up of the group members. They each unwittingly or with knowledge take on a certain character. There is always the devil's advocate, the sceptic, the nonconformist, the disgruntled, the optimistic, the pessimistic, the team player, the director, and the crew. The set design can be an office, board room, church, house, or any place where people can gather to form a ensemble. The script contains the mission and objectives of the group but there is usually another version in the form of a hidden agenda somewhere off stage. The staging is done by the creator of the group with the help of the director and a few loyal stage hands. There are always individuals willing to upstage the director if given an opportunity. The props are the behaviours, attitudes, image, egos, insecurities, preconceived notions, openness, hopes, and fears. With all of this going on behind the scenes, as the group carries out its task, the play is changing as the drama unfolds making communication an art worth cultivating. The lighting effect appears clearer as the characters reveal their true feelings. To become a better team player it is important to understand how to communicate and relate to other team members while recognizing that some of the acting is a part of a continuing saga called interpersonal relations. To receive rave reviews, the first place to start is in Listening: The Heart of Communication.

4. Listening: The Heart of Communication

One of the hardest, yet most important skills is to be a good listener. Why is it so difficult to listen? There are several reasons but this one is the most prevalent: we can't wait to tell our side of the story, how we feel, and what we think. It is human nature to want to express ourselves or to tell others how to live their lives. In a fast-paced world where our attention span is short, it is sometimes painful to have to stop and listen to what someone has to say. This is especially true if we are not really interested.

An Illustration

I remember having lunch with a friend where I probably got one word in throughout the whole meal. She had no commas, semi-colons and definitely no periods in any of her sentences. It was a real art how she was able to eat and talk at the same time without making a mess. But she did it. I went through several emotional changes as I sat there waiting to at least answer some of the questions she had asked. I went from feeling interested in hearing about her, to anxious that I was not able to speak, to angry that she was so self-centred she did not even want to hear about me or my opinion and to empathetic because she really needed to be heard.

I had not seen her in a long time and could not recall her monopolizing the conversation to such a degree. I have seen her three times since and she is still the same. I have a choice to tell her how I feel about the one-way conversation (even though I couldn't get a word in edge-wise to tell her) or stop seeing her. I decided I would have lunch with her again when I didn't feel like talking, but didn't mind listening. In all seriousness, a complaint that is said quite often is people do not listen. They comment before they have heard the whole presentation.

People interrupt one another and some even walk out on a speaker because he talks too long. What is too long? I was told that 10 minutes was too long to talk to a group. If listening is the heart of communication, it is no wonder that conflicts and social crisis are increasing. How can we understand if we don't listen? When people do listen they do so in several ways, a few are described below:

(1)   **Empathetic listening**. We place ourselves in the speaker's shoes. We feel what they are feeling and identify with their problems.

(2)   **Sympathetic**. We feel sorry or understand the speaker's situation but we do not necessarily identify with their plight.

(3) **Blame Listening**. We listen to find fault with what people are saying or to prove our point.

(4) **Listening but not hearing**. We listen but do not hear what the speaker is saying. We are preoccupied with our own interpretation of what they mean or refuse to recognize them as the author of their own thoughts and feelings.

(5) **Patronizing**. We listen with a sense of superiority and sometimes try to mask it by falsely appearing to care and understand.

(6) **Authority**. We listen but we know it all and before the speaker is through we have their problems all figured out and proceed to tell them what to do.

(7) **Mechanical**. We are experts at the technical aspect of listening and know when to nod, smile and say, ha ha, but in reality we are not listening.

(8) **Balloon**. We listen but are filling up to a point where we will burst if we don't get to comment.

(9) **Judge**. We listen but as soon as the person says something that we don't want to hear or is out of line in our minds, we make an out of order call.

(10) **Boiling Pot**. We listen but we are slowly seething underneath and therefore will not resolve anything. We leave or burst before the end of the conversation.

The problem with many of the ways in which we listen is that we are not working toward building understanding, improving relationships, or diversifying of information. Instead we limit our potential for effective communication with listening impairments. We listen:

Arrogantly

Patronizingly

Defensively

Prejudicially

Antagonistically

Confrontationally

Disinterestedly

Even if we do not say anything that would represent these listening impairments they are transmitted through our non-verbal styles. Our facial expressions, body language, and attitude are important communication indicators to what we are really feeling about a person or a situation. My mother used to tell me: "eyes do not lie." If you study people you will see physical indicators that demonstrate what they are feeling when there words say otherwise. I recall being pulled over by a police officer for speeding. I had my car on cruise control and knew it couldn't have been me. I believed that he had caught the car ahead on his radar screen but somehow he stopped me. I never knew what actually happened but I knew I had not exceeded the speed limit. I decided to exercise my right and I challenged my ticket in court. When the judge called my name, my heart began beating faster, I didn't realize how intimidating a courtroom could be until I was there representing myself. My husband gave me moral support. As I listened to the police officer's impressive presentation and examined his technical and comprehensive visual of the radar system, I felt like a dwarf in a field of giants. I wondered how was I going to convince anyone I was telling the truth. As I listened further I began to look at my accuser carefully. He was polished in his best officers' uniform and as I looked at his badge and then his hat sitting on the corner of an empty chair, I noticed his left hand. It was shaking badly. I thought I was the one that should be shaking with all of his fancy devices and technical jargon but I was not. Why was he? I took it to mean that he was covering the fact that he didn't really have a case and was trying to intimidate me. He was in fact the one intimidated. When it was my turn the judge asked me if I understood all of the technical information. I replied that with all due respect to the officer's elaborate description of the radar system, it failed to show that my car exceeded the speed limit and my car was not clocked on the screen. In fact it did not show any sign of my car having been present. The judge concurred. I won the case. Body language, self-control, and effective listening can be important allies when faced with challenging situations.

5. Consequences of Blame and Guilt

A flower cannot grow if it's condemned to die. When our personal skills are underdeveloped we bring unhappiness to ourselves and others. We also limit our ability to build an inner light which can draw those we love closer. Have you seen couples who spend so much time blaming each other that they never deal with the underlining issue which could resolve their problem? When people place blame, it puts someone else on the defensive and results in guilt or denial which undermine the spirit of co-operation and understanding. This is especially evident in romantic relationships. Learning to balance our responsibility while maintaining our self-respect is a challenging goal when interacting with people. A positive self-esteem allows us to admit when we are wrong. It gives us the strength to make needed changes and then to move on without the fruitless feeling of guilt. Guilt can be an indicator that you must deal with an issue or person in a more effective manner, but, it should not be an ongoing disposition. It can be a destructive feeling that can paralyse your mind and thus prevent you from addressing the real issues.

Unfortunately, guilt is used as a teaching tool by many parents, teachers and other educators. Our parents teach what was taught to them and this continues a circle of negative inner conditioning. To break this pattern we sometimes must do it for ourselves. We have to acknowledge that how we learned was not positive for our development and understanding of who we are. Our parents did what they thought was right or were limited in their ability to face their own problems. We need to encourage ourselves to stop self-defeating behaviour and begin a concerted program to break negative attitudes. Placing guilt is not a productive means of making a person feel or change. Instead it makes an individual feel unacceptable and unworthy. It places too much emphasis on the individual's mistake and not enough on the person's inner development. It also places one person as the judge and another as the criminal. This divides people instead of bringing them closer. In diversity-training for example, I have found that making people feel guilty for racial or sex discrimination is not effective in the long run. The person will spend much time trying to prove he or she is not the cause of the problem and will retreat into a patronizing, "I'm sorry for your pain" attitude when really they do not understand or care about another's plight. Other times people are in total denial that a problem exists and will in turn blame the person who is being prejudiced against.

There is a difference between responsibility and blame. Responsibility says we can make a difference and take leadership in eliminating a problem like racial discrimination as opposed to blame which says you caused the problem and you are at fault, you should feel guilty and ashamed.

The substantive and productive task of problem-solving will not be addressed in an atmosphere where blame and guilt prevail. Instead, a forum must be created where an honest and serious effort can evolve where a strategic plan is designed to address the issue. This approach is valid for other concerns. Without tangible goals and a commitment, progress will be too slow or not forthcoming. In any human relationship we must learn to question and seek the truth in a way that encourages openness and honesty to bring about co-operation and understanding. Learning to build effective communication is not about ignoring a deceitful or harmful act which resulted in pain for someone. It is the process whereby a resolution can be developed for the good of all involved. This will encourage personal growth as opposed to destruction. As the 35th president of the US, John F Kennedy once said, "Let us never negotiate out of fear but let us never fear to negotiate." It is through this philosophy that real progress can be made.

Six Tips to Eliminating Blame and Guilt When Communicating

1. Keep focused on the problem rather than the person. Stop yourself if you begin to name-call or bring up an event from the past for the purpose of hurting others.

2. Take responsibility for your own faults.

3. Work on finding a resolution that is fair, thoughtful and empathetic.

4. Share your pain or hurt without accusing or blaming another. In sharing your pain, explain why you feel the way you do and how you want to get rid of this pain. In other words deal with the action, not the person. For example say: "I really feel unappreciated when I am the one always calling," instead of: "you make me feel so bad when you do not call me."

5. Listen before you speak to try and understand the other person's point of view. Do not interrupt or argue that they are wrong. If you listen first then they will feel more like listening to you. When you do talk do not refute or argue what they have said,

instead discuss your reasons for feeling the way you do.

6. Summarize what the other has said and they in turn should summarize what you have said. Share four positive traits you find in the other person. Ask them in turn to share four positive traits about you. Then together begin to work on the ways you can deal with your respective problems, determining solutions, and how you can build up the positive aspect of your relationship.

6. Resolving Conflict by Creating a Win/Win Situation

It takes two to fight but only one to find a solution. But two have to agree on it so that it becomes a resolution. One of the biggest challenges in personal achievement is the skill of resolving conflict and creating a win/win situation for all involved. This is difficult because it takes emotional maturity, a fairness mentality, and a belief that there is more to winning than to someone else losing. Resolving conflict entails four major elements:

(1) **Understanding the problem.** In many conflicts there are extenuating circumstances that drive the interaction, resulting in the real problem going undetected or lost along the way. People build cases based on their own needs which often has nothing to do with the issue at hand. It is important to make sure that you understand the problem from the other person's perspective.

(2)   **Repeat what you have heard.** When you think you have understood the problem it is important to repeat it back so that the other person knows that you have heard their concern correctly.

(3)   **State your case.** After you have listened and opened to the other viewpoint, state your issue as clearly and non-aggressively as possible.

(4)   **Consensus Building.** Examine the problem (not the person) and form an agreement on the issues. Determine the rules for agreeing to disagree without being disagreeable.

(5)   **Creative Bargaining.** Find out what it would take for the person to find a resolution to their problem or concern. Then state what it would take for you to find a resolution to your problem or concern. The final step is for each to select what they could do to resolve the issue so that each party can move closer to receive what they wanted without the other person having to lose totally in the process.

Conflict occurs when emotions are high and the object of the discussion is to win at all costs. People do not usually uncover the real problem and then spend hours exerting power plays, protecting egos, and trying to convince others to give in to their demands. There are also times when the other person's agenda may not be to find a win/win resolution but to cheat you.

I was in a situation where a business organization wanted to form a partnership with our company. We spent days sorting out the details of the potential joint-venture. We were interested in combining forces with a well-established company as we were still building up our company at the time. However, we soon learned that the other organization saw us as an opportunity to make money from us without effort. As we studied the arrangement, it was obvious that we would do the work, generate the business, give the seminars and prepare the materials. They would help as they saw fit but would take a percentage on all profits. Something was certainly wrong with this picture. After additional discussions, it was evident that they did not want to compromise. Their goal was not to work with us, it was to use us. Our aim was to always leave a business discussion on a high note even when the outcome was not positive. When they learned that we were not so hungry that we would accept anything, they abruptly and impolitely ended our talks. Although we were displeased with their approach and for the time wasted, we felt it was a good experience and sent them a polite note thanking them for their time and interest in working with us. It is always better to leave with class and never close a door you may have to walk through again.

Building co-operation is another personal achievement. When you can get people excited about a goal and create environments that are conducive to positive interactions and effective communication, you have contributed greatly to the endeavour.

Co-operation is based on respect, openness, trust and integrity. These conditions generate a willingness among people to come together to complete a task. So often people try and build teams but neglect the underlining conditions that make a team work in the first place. Jim, prided himself on being a team-building expert. He had energy and the gift of persuasion. He dreamed of travelling the world telling people how to build and manage high-performance teams. The problem was that although Jim had high performers, and the appropriate resources to do so, he was unsuccessful in building such teams. He neglected to cultivate respect, openness, trust, and integrity. He violated these qualities needed to lead such an endeavour. He was so focused on the qualities the team needed that he forgot the qualities that he himself required. Jim hadn't involved any of his performers in the planning process. He chose a friend and future business partner to come into the company and lead the team-building sessions. He punished people indirectly when they were open and honest by setting them up to be challenged in future activities. He lost the trust of the group when he conspired with the outside consultant to use the sessions as a means of highlighting the perceived trouble-makers of the group. He showed he lacked integrity. He then fired the group that was committed to helping the team-members who had relationship problems, before the team process that a leader had diligently presented was even tried. The problem with managers like Jim is that they get carried away with the ideas and processes but do not practice what they preach. They don't "walk the talk".

Making a Difference

The following are three people who were my mentors in my early professional development and who exemplified the essence of EQ.

1. People Can Make a Difference

When a door is closed, God opens a window. I remember my first day on the job as a new teacher. I was full of energy and enthusiasm. I had received high marks as a student teacher and everyone on the staff liked me. I went from teacher to teacher and everything I said and did was wonderful. I believed that education was going to be my life's work and I was pleased that I had not pursued another career. It seemed as soon as my training wheels were off, and I became a full-fledged teacher and the real challenges were to begin. I was on a romantic high, in love with my own feelings of success.

What I began to observe was that my fellow teachers were not supportive in the same way that I had experienced during my student teaching. I found that my enthusiasm and energy were regarded negatively and dismissed as inexperienced frivolity. I became isolated and when I spoke at meetings teachers would ignore me or point out my lack of teaching years by making sarcastic remarks. I found myself alienated and realized my efforts were not appreciated. This was a blow to me. I began to see that some of the teachers were frustrated, apathetic, indifferent, and even held a dislike for their work. From those teachers who were motivated and still enjoyed their work, there was a tendency to feel threatened by the new kid on the block. They wanted to hold onto their position within the hierarchy and did not relish the thought of sharing power with a newcomer. I had entered the competitive arena and no longer would I be regarded as a bright, energetic young teacher— I was now a rival.

I was crushed at first because I thought it was me, I must have done something wrong. So I tried on different attitudes and behaviours, much like you would try on a hat. But I found none of them fitted and I felt phoney and flat. My various personality aliases were liked by some and disliked by others. After a while I would go back to being myself and almost feel guilty for letting down those who approved of my false self. I was being what others wanted but not the person I was meant to be. My family and friends told me it was like an initiation where you have to pay your dues. After a certain time I would be welcomed into the group. They counselled me that I should just be myself and in time all would be well and I would be the same star teacher I once was as a student. They hadn't told me that now the difference was that I had become a threat to those whose main objective was to stay ahead and at someone else's expense.

I have found that if the door is closed, God opens a window. During my six years of teaching I never gained entry into the elite group but established my own group and invited everyone to join. I met three people who will always remain pivotal to my earlier professional development. Alberta, was a dynamic and committed educator who truly loved teaching. She wasn't accepted by the core group because she was an advocate for students. She would verbally defend students in the teacher's lounge when someone was making fun of one of them. She would lecture on the important role we had been charged with. To those of us who really wanted to make a difference we found her to be enriching and wise. To those who had other interests she was a troublemaker and a bore. I learned from her the importance of maintaining your own ground and not becoming too consumed with the idea of belonging. It was our job to provide the best education for the students and the rest was inconsequential. Emily, as a teacher, was in a career that was created out of her own image. She exemplified the best in all of us. She was instrumental in helping me sharpen my skills as an educator. Her example inspired me to seek higher education and excel in my work in order to be of the best service to my students. Her unending support of me during challenging times was the torch that showed me the way. Emily believed that everyone was potentially gifted and if they were given the opportunity to shine they would. She believed totally in the human spirit and that we have the inner resources to overcome the worst adversity and the tenacity to find joy.

Dr Bob was an individual who exemplified emotional intelligence through his leadership and unending dedication to helping others. In him I found an early mentor who demonstrated through action the power of unselfishness and respect for human dignity which provided a model of leadership which I still hold to be true today. He always maintained that people were the most important factor in any situation. He would always say people come first and after that the rest will follow. He believed in a shared vision and gave credit to everyone but himself. He made people feel that they were very vital and he did humanitarian gestures very quietly with no need for recognition. He was a formidable debater in situations that called for decisions and he went up against the tide when necessary.

I learned that you can make a difference in a quiet way and this peaceful manner can produce the most thunderous result. In a world where who can scream the loudest is heard, his teachings emphasized that it's not who yells the loudest that counts but who can gather the mental and physical resources needed to accomplish the challenge. That he did time and time again.

At some point in each of our lives we will meet people who really make a difference and touch us in ways that will help us grow. The biggest tribute we may pay to our mentors is to give what we received to someone else along our journey.

Success is a word that is used to associate someone who has obtained something that we perceive as being difficult, yet we forget that we are already successful if we only allow our authentic self to break through the barriers we impose or the ones constructed by the outer world. Like my three mentors, there are people out there who have taken what they have and used it in the service of others. That in itself is an answer to our question of what is our purpose. Children are being asked to be much older than their years, and young adults are facing the same issues that the older generation must endure. Yet, for most of the older generation, it was a different world in which they grew up. The issues are now more diverse and intense. As a result young adults will need to be in touch with their inner core much sooner and work just as hard on their self-development as mature and experienced adults do in a career situation. Being wise is not only the luxury of the elderly. Young adults now have the wit and understanding on how to grasp the information important to their lives. Building personal skills as a lifetime endeavour will be helpful in enhancing our abilities to deal with challenges and to find peace and happiness. The importance of finding and maintaining a circle of mentors and supporters who will be honest and interested in helping us and whom we can in turn give help to is a key ingredient to our personal growth.

2.   Not Losing Sight of What's Important

When we reach the long awaited goal, we will have loved ones to share it with. Finally, as we create a personal purpose and go about preparing ourselves to meet our challenges and obtain our professional goals, let us not forget about the importance of people within our lives. So often we get caught up in the steps toward success, the destination, and the means, that we forget to get a life of our own. I have seen many successful people miserable inside because the money, power, and fame alone do not bring happiness because they did not have someone to share it with and did not think of themselves as a loveable person. To forget family and friends who were with us along the way or to neglect to cultivate meaningful relationships is a mistake that is made all too often. A natural prelude to developing and maintaining positive associations is to be the kind of individual that we would want as a friend. We must ask ourselves, would I want to be married to me? Would I want me as a friend? Would I want me as a parent? If the answer is no this is the time to make changes in your personal attitude, behaviour, belief, and priorities. The beauty of being human is that we can change. To better ourselves is a matter of desire, knowledge, and skill. Some of the answers are in this book and in others, but the action comes from within us. The processes that we use to accomplish a goal are the same we can apply to lead a happy and fulfilling personal life not only for ourselves, but for those people who love us. To believe in a higher power and to recognize the true meaning of life ends years of restlessness and searching. The realization that we have the inner resources to build a happy and productive existence should be a fact worth pursuing.

APPENDIX: EQ EXERCISES

R.E.A.C.T

What are Rational, Emotional, Actions for Creative Thinking?

This is a two-fold exercise called R.E.A.C.T. to help diffuse anger which leads to unproductive confrontations. It is useful to try this exercise before you confront someone, respond to a situation, or decide to leave a position because of internal hostility.

Technique—Part I

1. Find a quiet place away from the battleground.
2. Get a piece of paper and write across the top, "My Emotional Side".
3. Begin to write a letter to the person or object of your frustration. Write down all the things that have hurt you, made you angry, and that have bothered you.
4. Leave it until the next day or so. This will allow you an opportunity to release your anger, stress, and tension. For those people who prefer not to write use a tape recorder. It is wise not to mail the letter or the tape and to keep it hidden away until you have had time to cool down. After you have used it, it is best to destroy it. Usually when I have written My Emotional Side letter and then read it, the next

---

day, I immediately discard it because the intensity of my frustration has changed.

Technique—Part II

1. After you have written your emotional side letter get another piece of paper and write across the top, "My Rational, Creative and Thinking Side".
2. Start writing to yourself in the second person. You are now your own best friend.
3. Analyse the situation and your feelings from a non-judgmental way. Give advice about the problem as if you were giving it to your best friend.
4. Come up with the pros and cons of the action you think your friend should take.
5. Decide on a creative way to resolve the conflict and have your friend (actually yourself) come out on top.
6. Praise yourself and others that you are angry with for the things that they did well. Do not look at what they did wrong, you covered that in the emotional letter.
7. Leave the letter to reread the next day. Removing yourself from the situation and evaluating it from a friend or mentor's perspective will allow you to see things differently and rationally.

PERSONAL ACHIEVEMENT BALANCE SCALE

Identify the important components of your life—family, career, personal pursuits, money, and friends. Assign a value level code to each one: (1)

representing a high value, (2) representing a medium value, and (3) representing a low value.

Write down your high-value components in one column, medium-value components in a second column and low-value component in a third column.

Example

1=High Value	2=Medium Value	3=Low Value
family	money	civic duty
health	home	car
career	travel	material
friends	social	recreational
personal	interaction	sports
appearance	education	

Next to each value area (1=high, 2=medium, and 3=low) assess how much time and effort you spend maintaining and enriching each area. Think in terms of numbers—40 hours per week, 3 hours per week, etc. See the example below.

1=High Value	2=Medium Value	3=Low Value
family (18 hrs p.w.)	education (9 hrs p.w.)	civic duty (25 hrs p.w.)

Think about the feedback or signs that you receive regarding your efforts in each area. Does your spouse, children or friends complain about your lack of involvement? Do you have enough time to develop your interests or finish projects? Do you appear tired or depressed, etc?

If the time and effort you place is higher in the medium- or low-value ranges than in the high-value area, your priorities do not match your actions. Therefore you have misplaced your emphasis and you are out of balance with your priorities. You may want to reassess your priorities and set goals to assist you in achieving your priorities.

Periodically evaluate your priorities. Add new ones or eliminate the ones which have changed. Be sure to place the appropriate value next to each one and spend the appropriate time and effort cultivating each area. There will be times when your values are in conflict with one another. This is an opportunity to find creative ways to balance each one out without losing focus on immediate issues at hand. It takes skill in handling work and home but it can be done if we are willing to involve our families in planning quality-time together. Sometimes even family and friends can occupy us needlessly when we have something more important to do at the moment. So that we do not isolate our loved ones it is productive to schedule quality-time with them. This is also true for personal development activities and for getting needed rest and relaxation.

Food for Thought

1. Career-Planning Suggestions

Formulating a plan of action for making your dreams become a reality, is the time to be an innovative and visionary thinker. During this period if we become unimaginative or afraid our chances of stagnation are greater. It is at this time that we have an opportunity to stretch to new heights. The following are food for thought as you develop your career options:

1.   Do not panic when you have a setback. They are a necessary part in the growth process.

2.   Keep brainstorming. Creative thinking and talking with others will be a major way to uncover hidden opportunities. Someone or something will trigger an idea or path for you to follow.

3.   Be careful not to let the journey to success frighten you or make you lazy. The temptation to give up or to settle for anything rather than what you truly want will be present. Fight it unless you need to take time out to regroup before continuing to pursue your goals.

4.   You are in a game of career roulette, where you will take three steps forward—two back, one to the side—but eventually you will step into the arena you want, if you keep on target.

5.   Avoid placing stringent time limits for finding a new career, for example: I must leave my employment to seek another by 5 September. It is good to have a time-frame for where you want to move. But the importance is not so much the time but the steps that will ultimately lead you to your goal.

6.   Develop an action-oriented written plan which will take you step-by-step toward identifying the career you want.

7.   When you are in a toxic working environment, focus your attention to where you want to go, rather than dwelling on where you happen to be at the time or the place that you want to leave.

8.   By directing your energy on the end-result you will not allow current distractions to cloud your view or shape your confidence in a way that is counterproductive to what you ultimately want out of life. Look beyond a negative situation and use every setting, event, and interaction as an opportunity which will be useful to your future. Example: decipher if it is a learning possibility, or a chance to showcase your personal and professional skills, or will this person be able to help you? etc.

9.   Focus on the incremental steps of your career plan with specific outcomes in mind. For example, how are your promotional

materials (resume, etc)? Do you have a marketing strategy? Who are your competitors? Who are the key players? What resources will you need? Do you have a fallback plan?

10. Do not make people in your current professional arena more important than they are. Be sure to keep your perspective. During transition or turmoil your harmony can be shaken.

11. Recognize that when you undergo change you are in a vulnerable growth period. Be good to yourself. Share your frustrations with appropriate people but do not internalize or let your emotions get the better of you.

12. Discipline yourself to concentrate on the strategies you have created to accomplish your career goals. Periodic evaluations of your progress from a personal and professional point of view are productive. They give you a chance to alter your direction and improve your decision-making.

13. Remember to ask yourself questions when you are faced with decisions. Such as: how can this help me? Can I make this a win/win situation for all involved? What can I learn from this experience? What personal and professional skills will I need to overcome this?

14. An ongoing strategy of winners is to keep looking at the total picture. It is easy to get hung up on the sum parts and lose sight of the whole.

15. Recognize that failure and disappointment do not measure your overall ability. It is one indication of a needed improvement area. Winners do not let obstacles break their spirit, they use them as a means to succeed the next time around.

16. Keep in mind that there are many routes to reach your goal but the important thing to remember is to keep your faith, be joyous along the way and cultivate your skills so that you are ready when the opportunity is given to you.

2. When Accepting a Career: Issues and Questions to Consider

(Will it help?)	Vision direction
(What is the position?)	Current reality
(What will it do?)	Positioning
(Mobility?)	Opportunities-present/future
(Drawbacks?)	Cons (deficits)
(Advantages?)	Pros (plus)
(Returns)	Satisfaction level
(Stage of Development)	Timing

3. Four Inner Challenge Action Steps

The inner challenge in self-management is to focus our attention on organizing our potential vast internal voices, emotions, think processes, desires, along with our independent will to create a harmonious centre with components that each help us achieve success, happiness, and peace. The following are action steps which you can work on to help you deal with the challenges you face in your life.

A Screening Exercise

You have just received 100 different requests to give a presentation. You only have time for five speaking engagements. What do you do? How do you decide which ones to accept and which ones to reject? What is your rationale for doing so and what is your criteria for making your decisions?

See if your answers address any of the following suggestions:

1.   First, determine what is your goal in life, and what do you want to accomplish in giving your presentations.
2.   Second, identify and prioritize the needs of the requests being made.
3.   Third, who or what is your target and the reasons for your choices.
4.   Four, are your outcomes beneficial to yourself as well as others.

CREATING YOUR OWN SCREENING PROCESS (COMPLETE)

As you screen the information you receive keep in mind these questions:

- What are the important things in my life?
- What are the least important?
- What is productive to focus on, and what is not?
- What do I dwell on that is now outdated?
- What is holding me back from personal growth?
- Will this new knowledge help or hurt me?

SELf-MANAGEMENT PLANNING CHART

Think of a stressful situation you will have to face, look at the sample as a reference for filling in the chart on your own and use it as a reference for dealing with the situation.

stressful event	hot buttons	logic to use	emotion needed
breaking off a relationship	people who blame	reasoning	empathy
reprimand	tension	rational	self-control

1. CREATIVE PROCESS

Event One: Letting the person know that it is your need for change and growth that is the reason for the break-up and is not based on them alone. This puts the ownership on you without having to blame the other person or wait to have them blame you.

Event Two: In this situation, being aware that anger is a weak point for you means it is important to use positive self-talk that will emphasize the importance of learning from the experience, as opposed to feeling a loss of self-esteem. Maintaining self-control will enable you to be flexible in your response, opening a wider range of opportunities for growth than exerting more anger would allow.

Look back on the situation and answer the following questions as to how you could have handled the situation better:

1. What inner resources were needed to deal with the situation?

    _____

    _____

    _____

    _____

2. Where were you strong? Where were you weak?

    _____

    _____

    _____

    _____

3. What emotional response did you give?

_____

_____

_____

_____

4. Did it complement or conflict with your reasoning mind?

_____

_____

_____

_____

5. Intuiting would have helped me to ...?

_____

_____

_____

_____

6. Logic and analysis would have given me ...?

_____

_____

_____

_____

7. Imagination and creativity would have given me ...?

_____

_____

_____

_____

8. Emotion could have better been expressed if I had ...?

_____

_____

_____

_____

P.R.O.F.F SYSTEM

(Patience, Responsibility, Ovation, Follow-through, Faith.)

The P.R.O.F.F. system includes five elements. As you prepare to deal with a problem or a challenge complete the following strategy form:

1. How can I demonstrate my patience in meeting this challenge?
2. What is my responsibility and what resources do I need?
3. How can I give myself an ovation for the hard work that I put into meeting this challenge?
4. What follow-through is needed to maintain the progress made or to move forward with the situation?
5. In what ways can I maintain faith in myself and how can I work with others to achieve our goal?

EQ: The Key to Success
other exciting titles in the series

EQ SERVICE WITH A HEART
achieving EQ for outstanding customer service

"What is missing in customer service today? Heart!"

EQ LEADERSHIP SKILLS
for empowerment and change

"Why can some leaders balance their head and heart in the workplace, while others fall short and even fail?"

THE FOUNDATION
for personal and professional success

"Emotional intelligence is the basic foundation for building relationships and empowering self and others to overcome challenges—it is the balance between heart and mind."

EQ DEVELOPMENT
from success to significance

"People who have gone from success to significance know their value as a person, have meaningful relationships and can help cultivate the best in others. They have achieved harmony in their lives, allowing them to face adversity with optimism."

BUILDING POSITIVE RELATIONSHIPS
a pathway to happiness and prosperity

"The problem with relationships today is that we have not learned how to live with our own moods and emotions enough to harmonize with someone else."